An Introduction to Arbitration; A Guide for Students, Lawyers, and Everyone Else.

I0479251

Contents

Introduction..2

Chapter 1. Arbitration between two private individuals. 3

Chapter 2. Arbitration is regulated by the court. 4

Chapter 3. Beginning the arbitral process. 5

Chapter 4. When arbitration is needed. 6

Chapter 5. Disputes. 7

    5.1. Arbitration for commercial disputes..7

    5.2. Arbitration for the Construction Industry...8

    5.3 Arbitration for Labor Disputes. 9

    5.4 Arbitration for International Disputes. 10

    5.5 Arbitration for Consumer Disputes..11

Chapter 6. Mediation in Law. 13

Chapter 7. The difference between Arbitration and Mediation..14

Chapter 8. Types of Mediation. 15

    8.1 Facilitative Mediation...16

    8.2 Evaluative Mediation 16

    8.3 Transformative Mediation 17

    8.4 Narrative Mediation 18

    8.5 Online Mediation 18

    8.6 Court-ordered mediation. 19

Chapter 9. The Advantages of Arbitration in the Legal World..21

Chapter 10. The Disadvantages of Arbitration in the Legal World. 22

Chapter 11. Disputes that cannot be settled by arbitration...23

Chapter 12. Arbitration Agreements. 24

Chapter 13. Arbitration in the USA. 25

    13.1. History of Arbitration in the USA. 26

    13.2. Open-source Platforms for Arbitration...28

        13.2.1 A few open-source platforms for arbitration. 28

    13.3. The Federal Arbitration Act (FAA), the United States Arbitration Act of 1925............29

Chapter 14. Contract Arbitration Law. 30

Chapter 15. Practical Labor Arbitration..31

    15.1. The practical application of labour arbitration involves several steps. 32

Chapter 16. Interest Arbitration and Grievance Arbitration. 33

Chapter 17. Judicial Arbitration 34

Chapter 18. Securities Arbitration 35

Chapter 19. Government-supported Arbitration clauses. 36

    19.1. Enforcement of Arbitration Clauses 37

    19.2. The Validity of Arbitration Clauses is being tested. 37

    19.3. The modification of an Arbitration Clause...38

    19.4. The right to arbitrate can be waived. 39

Chapter 20. Excessive Arbitration Fees 40

Chapter 21. The Arbitration Tribunal. 41

Chapter 22. The Arbitral Tribunal Process. 42

Chapter 23. The appointment process at the beginning of arbitration..44

Chapter 24. Arbitration Umpire or Chairperson. 45

Chapter 25. The role of the Arbitrator Advocate...47

Chapter 26. The removal of the Arbitrator..48

    26.1. The Resignation of the Arbitrator 48

    26.2. The Death of the Arbitrator. 49

    26.3. Appointing a New Arbitrator after the Resignation or Death of the Previous One........50

    26.4. The Arbitrator Has Immunity from Being Sued. 51

    26.5. The Jurisdiction of the Arbitral Tribunal. 52

    26.6. The Arbitral Hearing Proceedings. 52

    26.7. Duties of the Arbitral Tribunal. 53

    26.8. The Procedure for the Arbitration Session. 54

    26.9. It is possible to appeal against an Award that was given by the Arbitral Tribunal. 56

    26.10. Specialized Arbitration Organizations...57

    26.11. Fees and expenses of an Arbitral Tribunal...58

    26.12. The American Arbitration Association, AAA and ADR (Alternative Dispute Resolution Services) 59

    26.13. The FMCS organization of the USA. The Federal Mediation and Conciliation Service. 59

Chapter 27. International Arbitration..61

Chapter 28. International Bar Association and Arbitration. 62

Chapter 29. The History of International Arbitration 63

Chapter 30. The Convention on the Recognition and Enforcement of Foreign Arbitral Awards; Enforcement of Arbitral Tribunal Awards in a Global Context. 64

Chapter 31. Interstate Arbitration. 65

Chapter 32. Arbitration in England. 66

Chapter 33. The History of Arbitration in England. 67

Chapter 34. The London Court of International Arbitration. 68

Chapter 35. International Chamber of Commerce. 69

Chapter 36. ICC Commercial Crime Services (CCS) 70

Chapter 37. Business Action to Stop Counterfeiting and Piracy (BASCAP) 71

Chapter 38. Business Action to Support the Information Society. 72

Chapter 39. National Academy of Arbitrators. 74

Chapter 40. Arbitration in Europe. 75

Chapter 41. Arbitration in Germany. 77

Chapter 42. Arbitration in France 79

Chapter 43. Arbitration in Italy. 81

Chapter 44. Arbitration in Spain. 83

Chapter 45. Arbitration in Portugal. 85

Chapter 46. Arbitration in Poland. 87

Chapter 47. Arbitration in Belgium. 88

Chapter 48. Arbitration in the Netherlands. 89

Chapter 49. Arbitration in Switzerland. 91

Chapter 50. Arbitration in Russia. 93

Chapter 51. Arbitration in China. 94

Chapter 52. Arbitration in Australia and New Zealand. 95

Chapter 53. Arbitration in Canada. 96

Chapter 54. Arbitration in the Arab world. 97

Chapter 55. Arbitration in Africa and South Africa. 98

Chapter 56. Arbitration is becoming more expensive. 100

Chapter 57. Steps to be taken to reduce the cost of arbitration. 101

Chapter 58. Alternatives to Arbitration. 103

Conclusion 105

Introduction

Arbitration is a very helpful tool, used all over the world. It is wise to get to know more about arbitration, you can save a fortune in legal expenses.

A disagreement between two or more parties is settled through arbitration by a neutral third party known as an arbitrator. Instead of proceeding to court, the parties agree to arbitrate their dispute, and they also agree to accept the arbitrator's ruling as final and binding.

When parties in a commercial dispute desire to avoid the expense and inconvenience of going to court, arbitration is frequently used. Together with other sorts of conflicts, it is employed in labor disputes, construction disputes, and others.

The arbitrator renders a decision after hearing the parties' arguments and supporting evidence during the arbitration process. An award is what the arbitrator decides, and it has legal force and effect just like a court ruling.

Depending on the parties' agreement, different rules and processes may apply when conducting the arbitration. For instance, although some arbitration processes permit evidence discovery, others do not. The qualifications and selection procedure for the arbitrator may also be outlined in the regulations.

I hope this book will be helpful and interesting to you. I was written in everyday language without too much legal jargon and technical details.

Chapter 1. Arbitration between two private individuals.

In the legal process known as arbitration between two private parties, a disagreement between the parties is settled by an arbitrator rather than by a judge. When parties to a contract or agreement with an arbitration clause disagree, this sort of arbitration is frequently used.

In private arbitration, the disputing parties' consent to the arbitrator's hearing of their case and to the arbitrator's ruling being final and binding. An award is what the arbitrator decides, and it has legal force and effect just like a court ruling.

Depending on the parties' agreement, private arbitration can be performed in accordance with a variety of norms and guidelines. The qualifications and selection process for the arbitrator, as well as the steps for presenting evidence and arguments, can all be outlined in the rules. Private arbitration is an alternative to court proceedings that can be less formal and more affordable. It can be done in person or online.

It's crucial to remember that private arbitration might potentially have drawbacks. The arbitrator's judgment might not be appealable, and the parties would have less control over the process and outcome than they would in court. Furthermore, private arbitration agreements could restrict the parties' access to the courts or their participation in class actions or other forms of mass litigation.

Chapter 2. Arbitration is regulated by the court.

The courts have jurisdiction over arbitration for a number of reasons. One of the primary justifications is to ensure that the arbitration process is fair and compliant with the law.

For instance, courts may get involved in arbitration to determine whether the arbitrator is competent enough and has the authority to settle the dispute. Courts also have the power to examine decisions to ensure that they follow the law and public policy, as well as to enforce arbitration agreements and judgements.

Courts may also participate in arbitration to provide oversight and ensure that the arbitration process is conducted fairly and impartially. For instance, courts may intervene in arbitration cases to address problems like bias, inappropriate conduct, or irregularities in the procedure.

To ensure arbitration upholds the public interest, courts may also be involved in regulating it. Establishing procedural rules for arbitration hearings, protecting the parties' interests, and ensuring that arbitration is a workable alternative to litigation could all be included in this.

Finally, courts' control of arbitration aims to promote fairness, consistency, and the public's interest in settling disputes outside of the standard judicial process.

Chapter 3. Beginning the arbitral process.

Depending on the rules and procedures that apply to the specific arbitration, different steps may be required to begin the arbitration process. Here are some general actions you can take to start an arbitration process, though.

Examine the arbitration provision or agreement. Review the conditions to understand the arbitration procedure and obligations if you have signed a contract or agreement that contains an arbitration clause.

Select a supplier for arbitration. It may be necessary for the parties to select an arbitrator depending on the terms of the agreement. One institution that may be contacted for arbitration is the American Arbitration Association (AAA).

Start the arbitration process. Normally, the party initiating the arbitration must notify the opposing party or parties in writing. A description of the issue and a request for arbitration should be included in the notice.

Choose a mediator. The arbitrator may need to be chosen by the parties themselves or in accordance with a process. Rules for choosing an arbitrator may also be set forth by the arbitration service.

Prepare your case, then submit it. The parties must prepare and submit their case after the arbitrator has been chosen. This can entail offering proof, papers, and witness testimony.

Participate in the arbitration hearing. The parties will be given the chance to present their cases at a hearing that the arbitrator will set. The hearing can take place in person or online.

Get the arbitrator's ruling. The arbitrator will deliver a written ruling, known as an award, following the hearing. The judgment will be definitive, enforceable in court, and binding.

It's vital to remember that the particular procedures and conditions for starting an arbitration process can change depending on the terms of the arbitration provider's agreement and its rules.

Chapter 4. When arbitration is needed.

When parties to a disagreement are unable to resolve their differences through dialogue or other means, arbitration may be necessary in a number of circumstances. Here are a few situations in which arbitration might be suitable:

Commercial disagreements. Business conflicts, such as those involving contracts, intellectual property, or employment agreements, are frequently settled by arbitration.

Construction-related disagreements. Arbitration is frequently used to settle disputes about payment, delays, and flaws in construction projects between contractors, subcontractors, and property owners.

A quarrel at work. Employers and employees who are involved in labor disputes, such as those involving salaries, benefits, and working conditions, frequently use arbitration to resolve their differences.

International controversies. As it can offer a neutral forum free from the laws and authority of any one country, arbitration can be used to settle conflicts between parties from various nations.

Consumer disagreements. Arbitration is occasionally used to resolve consumer disputes, including those involving warranties, product flaws, or services.

In general, arbitration may be appropriate in any circumstance where the parties to a dispute have agreed to settle their differences through a third-party neutral arbitrator and the dispute is not so significant or complex as to necessitate resolution through the courts or other formal legal processes.

Chapter 5. Disputes.

5.1. Arbitration for commercial disputes.

Disputes between corporations, as well as other economic conflicts, are frequently resolved through arbitration. The following are important considerations for commercial dispute arbitration.

A written agreement. Arbitration is frequently used to settle disagreements that result from a written contract between the parties. Commercial contracts frequently contain an arbitration clause that details the process and regulations of arbitration.

Selecting the arbiter. The chance to select an arbitrator with knowledge of the particular conflict field, such as construction or intellectual property, may be available to the parties in commercial arbitration.

Confidentiality. Most commercial arbitration hearings are private, so neither the specifics of the dispute nor the arbitrator's ruling are made public.

Efficiency and quickness. As opposed to going to court, arbitration can be a quicker and more effective approach to settle business issues. The arbitration hearing may usually be scheduled at a time that is convenient for both parties, and it may proceed more quickly than going through the legal system.

Enforceability. Courts can typically enforce arbitration awards, thus if necessary, the parties may do so to have the arbitrator's decision upheld.

Nevertheless, because arbitration is frequently quicker, more adaptable, and less expensive than going to court, it can be a valuable way for resolving commercial conflicts. To make sure that any arbitration agreement offers a fair and efficient method of resolving disputes, it is crucial to thoroughly evaluate its provisions before entering into one.

5.2. Arbitration for the Construction Industry.

In the construction sector, arbitration is a frequent form of dispute resolution since it can be a quicker, more adaptable, and more affordable alternative to going to court. Here are some essential considerations for arbitration in construction disputes.

A written agreement. Arbitration is frequently used to settle disagreements between the parties to a contract, such as a building contract. Such contracts frequently contain an arbitration clause that details the rules and steps involved in arbitration.

Choosing an arbitrator. The chance to select an arbitrator with knowledge of construction law or a related profession, like engineering or architecture, may be available to the parties in construction arbitration.

Seasoned witnesses. In construction arbitration, parties frequently call on experts to testify in regard to technical issues, such as building codes, design requirements, or construction standards.

Efficiency and quickness. Instead of going to court, arbitration can be a quicker and more effective option to settle construction issues. The arbitration hearing may usually be scheduled at a time that is convenient for both parties, and it may proceed more quickly than going through the legal system.

Confidentiality. Construction arbitration hearings are typically private, thus the specifics of the conflict and the arbitrator's ruling are kept private.

Enforceability. Courts can typically enforce arbitration awards, thus, if necessary, the parties may do so to have the arbitrator's decision upheld.

Overall, arbitration may be a good way to settle construction disputes because it offers a more specialized and time-saving process than going to court. To make sure that any arbitration agreement offers a fair and efficient method of resolving disputes, it is crucial to thoroughly evaluate its provisions before entering into one.

Employers and employees frequently use arbitration to settle labor issues. Here are some important considerations for the arbitration of labor conflicts.

Pacts for collective bargaining. Disputes arising under collective bargaining agreements (CBAs) between employers and labor unions are frequently resolved through labor arbitration. The arbitration clause in these contracts usually outlines the process and rules to be followed.

Choosing an arbitrator. The possibility to select an arbitrator with knowledge of labor law or a related area, such as employment law or human resources, may be available to the parties in a labour arbitration.

Complaint processes. Labor arbitration is frequently utilized to settle disputes brought by employees or the union under the CBA. A grievance process will normally be outlined in the CBA and must be fulfilled before arbitration may begin.

Efficiency and quickness. Instead of going to court, arbitration can be a quicker and more effective alternative to settle labor issues. The arbitration hearing may usually be scheduled at a time that is convenient for both parties, and it may proceed more quickly than going through the legal system.

Confidentiality. The facts of the disagreement and the arbitrator's judgment are typically kept private throughout labor arbitration hearings because of this.

Enforceability. Courts can typically enforce arbitration awards, thus if necessary, the parties may do so to have the arbitrator's decision upheld.

Overall, because it can offer a more specialized and effective approach than going to court, arbitration can be a valuable method for settling labor issues. To make sure that any arbitration agreement offers a fair and efficient method of resolving disputes, it is crucial to thoroughly evaluate its provisions before entering into one.

5.4 Arbitration for International Disputes.

International conflicts, including those involving parties from different nations or cross-border transactions, are frequently resolved by arbitration. The following are important considerations for international dispute arbitration.

Law and jurisdictional choice. The law that will apply to the arbitration and the venue may both be chosen by the parties in international arbitration. This may be crucial in order to guarantee that the agreement made will be upheld by the courts.

Selecting the mediator. The chance to select an arbitrator with experience in international law or a relevant area may be available to the parties in international arbitration.

Translation and language. Parties to international arbitration may come from several nations and speak various languages. The arbitration processes must be conducted in a language that all parties can understand, and translations must be made available as needed.

Recognition, implementation and enforcement. There should be widespread acceptance, use, and enforcement of international arbitration. International treaties and agreements between nations can help with this

Cultural variations. Parties to international arbitration may come from various cultural backgrounds with various legal structures and commercial practices. It's critical to be aware of these variations and to make sure that the arbitration process is carried out in a way that is just and considerate to all parties.

In general, arbitration can be a helpful technique for settling international conflicts since it can offer an impartial and effective procedure that is suited to the needs of the parties. To make sure that it offers a fair and efficient method of resolving disputes in a global environment, it is crucial to thoroughly evaluate the provisions of any arbitration agreement before entering into one.

5.5 Arbitration for Consumer Disputes.

Consumer arbitration agreements can be used to settle disputes, but it's vital to remember that consumer protection laws frequently review and regulate these agreements. Here are some essential considerations for arbitration of consumer disputes.

Agreements for consumer arbitration. Several consumer contracts have arbitration clauses that mandate that customers arbitrate problems with the business rather to taking legal action, such as agreements with banks regarding credit cards and agreements with telecommunications companies regarding mobile phone contracts. However, these agreements might place restrictions on class action lawsuits, which could make it challenging for customers to organize to pursue a claim.

Arbitration agreements' fairness. Agreements involving consumer arbitration are frequently examined to make sure they are just and do not prejudice consumers. For instance, courts may consider the agreement's clarity, whether the consumer had a real chance to reject the arbitration clause, and if the arbitration process would be too costly for the customer.

Regulations and practices. Consumer arbitration may follow different rules and procedures than other types of arbitration. To ensure a fair and effective process for resolving consumer disputes, the American Arbitration Association, for instance, has a set of Consumer Arbitration Rules.

Arbitration's legal obligations. Consumers may be reneging on their right to go to court and have a judge or jury hear their case because arbitration agreements are typically binding.

Legal options for redress. It is crucial to guarantee that customers have access to judicial recourse if arbitration is unable to settle their issue. Statutory damages and other remedies that are available in court but not in arbitration may be included in some consumer protection laws.

Overall, arbitration can be an effective way to settle consumer issues, but it's crucial to make sure that the arbitration agreement is fair and that customers can seek legal recourse if required. Before signing any arbitration agreement, consumers should carefully read it, and they may want to get legal advice to make sure their rights are safeguarded.

A mediator is a neutral third person who assists parties in a legal dispute in coming to a mutually acceptable arrangement. Mediation is a type of alternative dispute resolution. Although it can be utilized in criminal cases and other types of disputes, mediation is frequently used in civil matters including personal injury, employment, and family law situations.

The mediator's job is to help the parties communicate, find common ground and points of contention, and look into possible solutions. The mediator encourages agreement between the parties rather than making decisions on their behalf, unlike a judge or an arbitrator.

The parties are normally responsible for the mediator's fees, whether mediation is requested by the court or is voluntary. Compared to a trial, mediation is frequently quicker, less expensive, and gives the parties more influence over the result. A heated legal issue may also harm relationships between parties, which mediation frequently helps prevent.

Ultimately, mediation can be a useful method for settling legal issues and a good substitute for courtroom battles.

ADR alternatives like mediation and arbitration both have their advantages and disadvantages.

Mediation is a method. It is well-liked because it is usually inexpensive and brief. A mediator helps two or more parties in a disagreement come to a mutually acceptable arrangement. The mediator is an impartial third party. It's known as mediation. Instead of making decisions on behalf of the parties, the mediator helps them communicate and negotiate. The parties can decide whether to accept or reject the mediator's recommendations because mediation is frequently optional. In addition to often preserving connections between parties, mediation can be less official, less expensive, and more informal than arbitration.

In contrast, arbitration is a process where a neutral third party, known as an arbitrator, hears testimony and renders a decision on behalf of the parties. The arbitrator's decision, known as an award, is enforceable in court and is binding. Arbitration may be compulsory or optional, less formal than litigation but more formal than mediation. When the arbitrator makes the final decision, arbitration can be quicker and less expensive than going to court, but the parties have less control over the outcome.

In conclusion, the main distinction between mediation and arbitration is that mediation is a non-binding process that seeks to facilitate communication and negotiation between parties in order to reach a mutually acceptable agreement, whereas arbitration results in a binding decision made by a third party.

There are various forms of mediation, such as.

Efficient mediation. The most typical type of mediation is this one. In order to facilitate communication and enable the parties to come to a mutually agreeable agreement, the mediator serves as an impartial facilitator.

Mediator evaluation. In this kind of mediation, the mediator expresses their viewpoint on the situation and the expected result of a trial. The parties may be able to come to an agreement as a result.

Mediation that is transformative. The goal of this sort of mediation is to enhance the parties' relationship via improved communication and mutual understanding. The mediator assists the parties in recognizing and resolving underlying problems that may be causing the conflict.

Mediation using stories. In narrative mediation, the mediator listens to the parties' stories and then works with them to understand and reframe them. This may facilitate the parties' discovery of shared interests and resolution.

Internet negotiation. With the development of technology, mediation can now be carried out electronically, for as through video conferencing. Parties that are unable to physically attend a mediation session may find this convenient.

Mediation mandated by the court. Courts in certain jurisdictions order parties to try mediation before a trial. This may facilitate settlement and lessen the backlog in the courts.

The nature of the issue and the requirements of the parties involved will determine the sort of mediation that is used.

8.1 Facilitative Mediation.

A third person serves as the mediator in a form of mediation called facilitative mediation. He or she is responsible for assisting the parties to a disagreement in communicating and coming to a compromise. The mediator's job is to facilitate negotiations and assist the parties in determining their points of agreement and dispute.

The mediator does not voice their own judgment or make judgments on behalf of the parties in facilitative mediation. Instead, the mediator works to make the parties aware of one another's needs, interests, and viewpoints. The mediator helps the parties to communicate with one another, engage in dialogue, and come up with potential solutions.

Facilitative mediation can be used to resolve a number of conflicts, including those involving the workplace, the family, and business. It is an informal and adaptable approach that may be customized to the unique requirements of the parties. Facilitative mediation is frequently helpful in preserving relationships between parties that may be harmed by a contentious legal dispute and can be a cost-effective and expedient approach to resolve issues without going to court.

8.2 Evaluative Mediation

Evaluative mediation is a sort of mediation in which the mediator offers an assessment of the legal situations, taking into account both the advantages and disadvantages of each party. If the issue goes to trial, the evaluative mediator should attempt to determine what the likely result would be. Based on their assessment, the evaluative mediator may also make settlement suggestions.

Evaluative mediation is frequently employed in complex issues that the parties are unable to resolve on their own, in contrast to facilitative mediation, which focuses on discussion and negotiation between the parties. In evaluative mediation, the mediator is often an experienced lawyer or retired judge who is familiar with the legal problems raised by the case.

When the parties are unable to fully comprehend the legal issues at stake or have inflated expectations about how their case will turn out, evaluative mediation may be beneficial. The parties can make better settlement decisions if they have a better understanding of the advantages and disadvantages of their case thanks to the mediator's evaluation.

Although evaluative mediation is still a type of conflict resolution, compared to facilitative mediation, it might be more combative. The mediator's job isn't to be impartial; instead, they should weigh in on the situation and suggest ways to resolve it.

8.3 Transformative Mediation

The goal of transformative mediation is to improve the connection between the parties to the conflict. The objective of transformative mediation is to assist the parties in improving their communication and understanding of one another, which may result in a change in the dynamics of their relationship and ultimately aid in the resolution of their conflict.

In transformational mediation, the mediator serves as a facilitator to assist the parties in recognizing and resolving hidden problems that may be a factor in their disagreement. The mediator assists the parties in effectively communicating, appreciating one another's viewpoints, and working toward a resolution that serves their needs and interests rather than offering advice or making decisions for the parties.

When there is a history of conflict or a relationship that has to be maintained or healed, such as in family or workplace issues, transformative mediation is frequently employed. The parties' willingness to engage in self-reflection and mutual understanding is essential to the process' success because it is voluntary.

While it tries to change the way, the parties engage with one another rather than just settling the present conflict, transformative mediation can be a potent instrument for bringing about long-term change in relationships. Transformative mediation can help to avert future disputes and foster a more positive, fruitful relationship between the parties by enhancing communication and fostering trust.

8.4 Narrative Mediation

The tales and narratives that underlie a conflict are the main focus of the mediation technique known as narrative mediation. In narrative mediation, the mediator assists the parties in exploring and reframing their respective narratives in a way that fosters empathy and understanding and may ultimately result in a resolution.

The narrative approach to mediation acknowledges that our stories influence how we perceive the world and the people in it, and that by questioning and rewriting those stories, we can open up fresh avenues for conflict resolution and change. In narrative mediation, the mediator assists the parties in identifying and exploring their underlying narratives as well as in searching for recurring themes or values that may serve as the cornerstone of an agreement.

The fact that the parties can construct fresh narratives and prospects for resolution rather than merely reviewing the conflict's history is one of the primary benefits of narrative mediation. The mediator may employ strategies like reframing, re-authoring, and externalizing to assist the parties in developing fresh perspectives and innovative solutions.

When there is a lot of emotion present or when the parties have strongly held opinions, narrative mediation can be especially helpful. Narrative mediation can create fresh opportunities for discussion and settlement by assisting the parties in reexamining their histories and points of view. It is frequently employed in domestic, social, and professional conflicts.

8.5 Online Mediation

Internet mediation, usually referred to as virtual mediation, is a procedure where parties to a dispute take part in a mediation session virtually, typically utilizing video conferencing software or other online communication tools. Internet mediation has grown in popularity over the past few years as a result of technological advancements and the expanding demand for remote dispute resolution.

Over in-person mediation, online mediation can have a number of advantages, including increased accessibility, convenience, and cost efficiency. Parties who live in different areas or who have demanding schedules that make it impossible to travel to in-person mediation sessions may find special benefit from online mediation.

Parties normally need a steady internet connection, a computer or mobile device with a camera and microphone, and access to video conferencing software or other online communication tools in order to engage in online mediation. In most cases, the mediator will collaborate with the parties to make sure that the technology is configured properly and that everyone feels at ease using it.

Similar to in-person mediation, the online mediation process involves the mediator serving as a third party impartial to facilitate communication, identify points of agreement and disagreement, and work toward a settlement. To support the process, the mediator may employ a range of tools and strategies, such as breakout rooms for private meetings and virtual whiteboards for solution-generating.

Online mediation has certain drawbacks even though it can be a very effective approach to settling disputes away. For instance, developing rapport and trust between persons who have never met in person may be more challenging. In other cases, technical difficulties or concerns with internet connectivity can also scuttle the mediation process. Yet, many parties have utilized online mediation to successfully settle their disagreements, and the technique is likely to spread in the coming years.

8.6 Court-ordered mediation.
A judge can require parties in a legal dispute to participate in mediation in order to settle their case without going to trial. This process is known as court-ordered mediation. Depending on the jurisdiction and the particulars of the case, court-ordered mediation may be either voluntary or required.

The judge may encourage or recommend that the parties in voluntary court-ordered mediation consider mediation as a means of avoiding trial, but ultimately the parties' decision to engage is up to them. Before a matter can move to trial, the judge must order mandatory mediation in which all parties must attend and make a sincere effort to settle their differences.

Court-ordered mediation seeks to persuade the parties to settle their differences amicably, which can save a full trial and save time and money. Because the parties can cooperate to find a resolution rather than having a judge impose one on them, mediation can also help to maintain relationships between the parties.

The parties often cooperate with a fair mediator who facilitates the discussion process and aids them in identifying points of agreement and dispute during court-ordered mediation. The mediator does not decide for the parties; instead, they are assisted in exploring their choices and coming to a compromise that satisfies their requirements and interests.

The details of any settlement reached through court-ordered mediation will be put forth in a formal agreement that is enforceable against all parties. The matter will move forward to trial as originally intended if the parties are unable to reach a settlement.

In the legal system, arbitration has many benefits, including.

Efficiency. Compared to regular court proceedings, which can be expensive and time-consuming, arbitration is frequently a quicker process. This is so that the arbitration can be shortened to concentrate on the main points of contention. The parties can also agree on the date, time, and location of the arbitration.

Expertise. Experts in their field, such as lawyers, businesspeople, or former judges, who have the expertise and experience necessary to comprehend the intricacies of the disagreement, are frequently used as arbitrators. As a result, they are able to make well-informed decisions that are based on the law and the relevant facts.

Flexibility. Because arbitration is a flexible process, the parties can customize the proceedings to meet their unique circumstances. They can come to an agreement regarding the arbitration's rules, language requirements, and venue.

Confidentiality. The facts of the dispute are frequently kept private during arbitration procedures since they are considered to be confidential. This may be crucial in business disputes when the parties may desire to safeguard their commercial interests or trade secrets.

Finality. The parties cannot appeal the verdict since arbitration awards are often final and binding. This might provide the conflict a sense of closure and finality, enabling the parties to get on with their personal or professional life.

In general, arbitration can be a quicker, more effective, and more affordable alternative to regular court proceedings for resolving disputes, especially when it comes to business conflicts. Along with giving the parties more knowledge and secrecy, it can also provide them more influence over the process and result.

Chapter 10. The Disadvantages of Arbitration in the Legal World.

In the legal community, arbitration also has some drawbacks, including.

Fewer possibilities for appeal. Arbitration judgments, in contrast to court processes, are typically final and binding, leaving the parties with few avenues for appeal. This could be a drawback if the arbitrator makes a mistake in law or fact or if fresh evidence surfaces after the award have been rendered.

Transparency is lacking. While maintaining anonymity may be beneficial in some circumstances, it can also be detrimental if it hides the process of resolving conflicts from the general public. This can erode public trust in the legal system and make it more challenging for others to comprehend how to work within it.

Costs. Arbitration is often more effective and less expensive than court processes, but it can still be pricey. Usually, the arbitrator's fees and any other related expenses for the arbitration must be covered by the parties. The parties may also need to retain the services of attorneys and other specialists to represent them in the arbitration.

Few discoveries. Contrary to court processes, arbitration may place restrictions on the parties' capacity to exchange information through the discovery process. Because of this, it could be more challenging to develop a case or fully comprehend the opposing side's viewpoint.

Public accountability is lacking. In contrast to judges, arbitrators are not publicly accountable and are not elected officials. If the arbitrator has a close relationship with one of the parties or if there are doubts about the arbitrator's credentials or behaviour, this may give rise to issues about impartiality.

Ultimately, arbitration has some disadvantages even though it may have some benefits in some circumstances. When choosing arbitration as their method of dispute resolution, parties should carefully weigh the benefits and drawbacks of the process.

Chapter 11. Disputes that cannot be settled by arbitration.

Due to their nature, some disputes cannot be settled through arbitration. Arbitration is not permitted in two main categories of legal actions. Procedures that produce decisions on which the parties cannot agree fall under the first category. Examples include court cases that have public or third-party implications or are handled in the public interest. These contains issues involving antitrust, criminal offenses, legal status, and family law. With a few exceptions, the majority of conflicts concerning private rights can, however, be settled by arbitration. For instance, because of the public registration system, an arbitration tribunal in a patent infringement case can only decide if a patent has been violated, not whether it is valid.

The second category of legal processes that cannot be arbitrated is those that are prohibited or limited by judicial decrees intended to safeguard more vulnerable members of the public, including consumers. For instance, German law forbids the arbitration of disputes involving the leasing of a dwelling because doing so may prejudice tenants. Similar to this, certain court orders demand that arbitration agreements with consumers be signed by both parties and only contain the arbitration agreement itself.

The best option for resolving conflicts may not always be arbitration, despite the fact that it is a flexible and effective alternative to judicial proceedings. In some situations, parties may choose to use the legal system to file a lawsuit in order to preserve their rights and ensure that the decision-making procedure is open and transparent. Additionally, it has been argued that the use of arbitration clauses in consumer and work contexts may restrict people's access to justice and deprive them of their legal rights.

Chapter 12. Arbitration Agreements.

Arbitration agreements are contracts that specify how disagreements between parties will be resolved through arbitration. These agreements come in two different varieties. both those signed after a dispute has developed and those that contain an arbitration clause. The former is more typical and can have legal implications in some nations. For instance, expenses may be shared by both parties in a standard arbitration clause in several Commonwealth nations but not in a submission agreement.

Arbitration clauses are typically upheld by the law due to the informality of the arbitration process, even if they lack the customary formal wording of legal contracts. Courts have upheld articles requiring arbitration in a specific location and under certain rules, as well as clauses saying that disputes will be resolved in accordance with principles other than those of a particular legal system.

Arbitration clauses are treated differently by the law. If it is established that an arbitration clause in a contract is unenforceable, it may also be deemed invalid. Yet, most courts will defer to the arbitration panel's judgment on the validity of the contract's arbitration clause. Although while concerns about fairness may arise in circumstances when a party is coerced into signing a contract that has a very beneficial arbitration clause, courts are often reluctant to interfere with the general rule that promotes economic expediency.

Chapter 13. Arbitration in the USA.

In the United States, arbitration is commonly used to resolve disputes in a wide range of industries, including construction, finance, and labor.

US customary arbitration practices.

Acceptance of Arbitration. The parties must concur to submit their dispute to arbitration, which is frequently voluntary. An agreement may be included in a contract or reached after a dispute.

Selecting a mediator. The parties may decide to have their dispute heard by a single arbitrator or by a panel of arbitrators. When the parties select an arbitrator, the appropriate area of expertise or past arbitration experience may be taken into account.

Arbitration procedures. The arbitration procedure might vary depending on the parties' agreement, although it frequently involves written submissions and an oral hearing. The arbitrator may issue a decision after considering the evidence and arguments presented by both parties.

Either enforceable or not. The parties may agree that the arbitrator's ruling shall be either binding or non-binding. A decision is considered binding if it is final and is upheld by a court.

Confidentiality. Since they are regarded as confidential, the details of the dispute and the arbitrator's decision are typically kept secret throughout the arbitration process.

Restricted rights to appeal. The alternatives available to parties to contest an arbitration ruling are often limited. This is done so that disputes can be resolved quicker and more successfully than they could be through traditional court-based litigation.

Arbitration is frequently used to resolve disputes in the USA because it can be quicker and less expensive than going to court. Arbitration does, however, have benefits and drawbacks, therefore parties should carefully consider their options before deciding whether to submit their dispute to arbitration. An agreement may be included in a contract or reached after a dispute.

13.1. History of Arbitration in the USA.

Since the beginning of the nation's legal system, there has been legal arbitration in the United States. By agreeing to have an impartial third party (the arbitrator) hear their case and render a ruling that is binding on all parties, parties to a legal disagreement can choose to resolve it through arbitration.

In colonial America, arbitration was employed to resolve disagreements between traders and merchants. The first federal arbitration statute was enacted by the Continental Congress in 1778, allowing for the arbitration of disputes involving ships and cargo acquired during the American Revolutionary War.

Arbitration became more popular in the United States as a mechanism of resolving conflicts between labor organizations and employers in the late 19th century. The first statute recognizing workers' rights to engage in collective bargaining and use arbitration to settle disputes was enacted by Congress in 1888.

In the 20th century, arbitration became increasingly popular, particularly in the context of business and international disputes. The Federal Arbitration Act, passed by Congress in 1925, created a framework for the legal enforcement of arbitration agreements and verdicts in the United States. The statute was created to promote arbitration as a viable and economical alternative to litigation. In the decades that followed, arbitration's acceptance increased, and it is now frequently utilized in a wide range of legal issues, including commercial conflicts, employment disputes, and consumer disputes. Nonetheless, there has been some debate in recent years over the use of arbitration, with detractors claiming that clauses in contracts requiring arbitration can restrict customers' rights to sue for damages in court.

Overall, the development of legal arbitration in the United States has been a reflection of the nation's long-standing dedication to settling legal disputes in a fair and unbiased manner, as well as of the shifting demands of American society.

Agreements to arbitrate were previously not regarded as legally binding under common law. This was based on a remark made by the renowned Lord Coke in the well-known Vynor Case in 1609, who said that either side could withdraw from an arbitration agreement.

Several merchants have started to disagree with this norm since the Industrial Revolution. They said that expensive, protracted court disputes were detrimental to corporate partnerships.

Arbitration was becoming more and more popular as a potential court litigation substitute.

In 1920, the New York Arbitration Act was created. The United States Arbitration Act was eventually passed in 1925. The Federal Arbitration Act is the name given to it now. With the exception of situations where fraud, unconscionability, or other conditions rendered the entire contract void, these rules created a framework to make arbitration agreements legally binding and enforceable. The Supreme Court intervened and expanded the reach of the FAA when the courts eased their standards for interpreting and applying interstate commerce. All of this took place throughout the 1980s and 1990s. Every aspect of interstate commerce was included. The Court's decision aimed to shield the general public from large corporations throughout the arbitration procedure.

It's important to note that there has been a growing trend in recent years calling for more justice and openness in arbitration hearings, particularly when it comes to disputes involving customers and employees. Mandatory arbitration clauses, which are frequently incorporated in contracts of adhesion, have been criticized for limiting people's access to justice and removing their power to sue corporations for misconduct. Several states have implemented legislation limiting the enforceability of obligatory arbitration agreements, while others have mandated that businesses provide consumers and employees with additional information about the arbitration process. Additionally, by utilizing the power of technology and community-driven governance, open-source arbitration systems increase the accessibility and affordability of arbitration.

13.2. Open-source Platforms for Arbitration.

Without using the traditional court system, parties can settle disagreements through an open-source arbitration platform in a fair, timely, and effective manner. In order to ensure that the arbitration is conducted in confidence and impartiality, the platform uses blockchain technology to generate a secure and tamper-proof record of all the proceedings.

The ability of parties to select their arbitrator(s) and modify the arbitration procedure to meet their needs is one of the main benefits of open-source arbitration. Its adaptability can facilitate faster and less expensive conflict resolution.

Anyone can utilize Open-source Arbitration, which was created by a group of legal and technological specialists. This indicates that the platform's source code is publicly accessible, and users are free to use it in accordance with the platform's policies.

Particularly in the case of complicated or transnational issues, open-source arbitration has the power to completely alter the way disputes are settled.

13.2.1 A few open-source platforms for arbitration.

Kleros. Kleros is a blockchain-based decentralized platform for dispute resolution that aims to provide a more open, safe, and affordable alternative to conventional arbitration. The platform is open-source.

Court of Aragon. A platform for decentralized dispute resolution based on the Aragon Network is called Aragon Court. It asserts that conflicts are resolved through a jury system, and that smart contracts are used to enforce the judgments. It is an open-source platform.

Codelegit. A system of jurors is used by the decentralized dispute resolution platform Codelegit to resolve conflicts. The platform is open-source.

Layer for Conflict Settlement. A platform dubbed Dispute Resolution Layer (DRL) is purported to enable parties to settle disputes through the use of so-called smart contracts. The platform is open-source.

Open-source systems' names and characteristics tend to evolve and change constantly. However, it may not be as simple to access these open-source platforms as is commonly suggested. Some platforms' source code may be accessible on GitHub.

I suggest exercising caution when using these open-source arbitration platforms. Although I have never used any of them, they may be quite useful.

13.3. The Federal Arbitration Act (FAA), the United States Arbitration Act of 1925.

A federal legislation in the United States that regulates arbitration agreements and awards is the Federal Arbitration Act (FAA). It is also called the United States of America Arbitration Act of 1925. The FAA was passed to promote the use of arbitration as a dispute resolution tool and to guarantee that arbitration agreements be upheld in both federal and state courts.

Arbitration agreements are generally enforceable under the FAA unless they are overturned, declared unlawful, or rendered otherwise unenforceable by state law. The FAA also provides for the confirmation and enforcement of arbitration awards, which means that unless there are grounds to vacate, alter, or correct the award, courts must recognize and uphold an arbitrator's decision.

One of the most important elements of the FAA is the requirement that, in cases where there is a valid arbitration agreement, judges stay litigation and order parties to arbitrate disputes. This means that if a dispute arises between parties who have already signed an arbitration agreement, the court may order that arbitration be used as a means of resolution rather than legal action.

All contracts involving interstate commerce, which includes the majority of business dealings, are subject to the FAA. There are a few exceptions, such as employment contracts for those working in transportation or contracts for the selling of securities.

The FAA has made a substantial contribution to the promotion of arbitration as a dispute resolution method in American courts. The implementation of forced arbitration clauses in consumer contracts and employment agreements, in particular, has drawn some criticism of the FAA in recent years.

Chapter 14. Contract Arbitration Law.

The legal framework guiding the arbitration process used to settle disputes between parties to a contract is known as contract arbitration law.

The following crucial elements often play a role in contract arbitration legislation.

Agreements for arbitration. Contracts may contain clauses mandating arbitration for the resolution of any disputes. The rules and procedures governing the arbitration process as well as the credentials of the arbitrator may be outlined in these agreements (s).

Procedures for arbitration. Depending on the regulations outlined in the arbitration agreement or the rules of the arbitration organization that the parties Decide to utilize, the arbitration process can change. These procedures may stipulate that evidence must be presented, arguments must be submitted, and arbitrators must be chosen.

Arbitration judgments. The arbitrator(s) will make an award at the end of the arbitration procedure that will decide how the dispute will be resolved. Depending on the provisions of the arbitration agreement or the laws of the jurisdiction where the arbitration is held, this award may be enforceable or void.

The execution of arbitration judgments. Binding While non-binding decisions may be the starting point for additional talks or legal action, binding awards may be enforced in court.

In general, the goal of contract arbitration law is to give parties to a contract a fair and effective way to settle disputes without having to resort to expensive and drawn-out judicial actions.

Alternative dispute resolution methods like labor arbitration are employed to settle conflicts between unionized workers and their employers. It is a procedure where a neutral, outside arbitrator is selected to render a definitive, legally-binding ruling about the disagreement.

When there is a collective bargaining agreement between the employer and the union that represents the employees, labour arbitration is frequently used. If negotiations or other channels fail to resolve an issue, it will often include a clause for labor arbitration.

The employer and the union normally agree on the arbitrator's selection in a labour arbitration case. After hearing arguments from both parties, the arbitrator will decide the case in a final and binding manner. The provisions of the collective bargaining agreement as well as any applicable laws and regulations are typically taken into consideration when the arbitrator makes a ruling.

Many conflicts, including those involving pay, benefits, working conditions, and disciplinary measures, can be settled by labor arbitration. It may also be employed to settle disagreements over the application or interpretation of collective bargaining agreements.

Comparing labor arbitration to regular court litigation, it is generally believed that labor arbitration is a more effective and economical means of settling conflicts. It makes conflict settlement quicker and potentially less expensive than going to court. Due to their input in choosing the arbitrator and defining the arbitration's rules, the parties to the dispute also have more influence over how it will be resolved.

A key instrument for resolving conflicts between employers and employees or labor unions is labor arbitration. It serves to maintain the stability and efficiency of the collective bargaining process and offers a fair and unbiased method of resolving conflicts.

15.1. The practical application of labour arbitration involves several steps.

Grievance resolution and negotiation. The parties must first negotiate and make an effort to settle the disagreement through the collective bargaining process before proceeding to labour arbitration. Employees and unions have the option of filing a grievance if they are unable to reach an agreement.

Choosing an arbitrator. If the dispute cannot be settled through normal negotiation, the parties must agree on an arbitrator. A neutral third party with knowledge of labor law and arbitration usually serves as the arbiter.

Conference prior to hearing. The parties may take part in a pre-hearing conference before the arbitration hearing. The arbiter will lay out the guidelines and processes that will be followed throughout the arbitration hearing process at this session.

Hearing in an arbitration. The parties must offer evidence, witnesses, and arguments to support their claims, just as in a trial. The arbitrator will evaluate the available data before reaching a final, conclusive determination.

Arbitration Decision. The arbitrator will publish an arbitration award, which is a written decision outlining the arbitrator's findings and conclusions, following the hearing. The arbitrator's ruling is final and binding, and the parties are required to follow it.

The execution of an arbitral award. The other party may attempt to have the arbitration judgment upheld in court if one of the parties refuses to abide by the ruling.

In general, the use of labor arbitration in daily life is a significant method of resolving conflicts between employers and employees or labor organizations. It helps to keep the collective bargaining process stable and effective by offering a fair and impartial method for resolving disagreements.

Chapter 16. Interest Arbitration and Grievance Arbitration.

Two types of labor arbitration that are frequently utilized in the process of collective bargaining are interest arbitration and grievance arbitration.

When the parties are unable to agree on the parameters of a new contract, interest arbitration is the mechanism used. A neutral third-party arbiter is chosen in this kind of arbitration to hear the arguments from both parties and reach a judgement on the specifics of the new contract after hearing all the evidence. The arbitrator's ruling, which could pertain to matters like pay, benefits, and working conditions, is typically conclusive and enforceable.

On the other hand, a process known as grievance arbitration is employed to settle disagreements on the interpretation and application of an existing collective bargaining agreement. A grievance can be filed if a union or an employee thinks the company has broken the terms of the contract. Normally, the dispute is settled through dialogue and, if required, arbitration. The arbitrator's ruling in this kind of arbitration is typically conclusive and enforceable.

In general, interest arbitration and grievance arbitration are crucial tools that support a fair and efficient collective bargaining process. They offer a way to settle disagreements that come up during the negotiating and application of collective bargaining agreements and support the upkeep of a solid and fruitful labor-management relationship.

Chapter 17. Judicial Arbitration

Court-based conflicts are settled by judicial arbitration, a type of alternative dispute resolution. It entails the selection of an impartial third party—typically a judge or an accomplished lawyer—to hear the arguments made by both parties and render a conclusive judgment.

In civil cases, judicial arbitration is frequently utilized to speed up conflict settlement and lighten the load on the court system. It is especially helpful when the parties can't reach a final agreement on their own but agree on a majority of the concerns.

When the parties decide to bring their disagreement to arbitration, the procedure of judicial arbitration usually gets started. After hearing both sides' arguments, the arbitrator will make a decision. Although in rare circumstances the parties may have the option to appeal the decision to a higher court, the ruling is typically conclusive and enforceable.

The fact that judicial arbitration is frequently quicker and less expensive than a trial is one of its advantages. However, because the parties have more sway over the arbitration process and frequently get to pick the arbiter who will hear their case, it may be more adaptable.

Ultimately, judicial arbitration is a valuable tool that can aid in the swift and fair resolution of conflicts. It is especially helpful in civil matters where the parties can reach a consensus on a majority of the issues but require the assistance of a disinterested third party to settle the remaining disagreements.

Chapter 18. Securities Arbitration

Conflicts between investors and their brokerage companies or financial advisors are resolved through securities arbitration. The Financial Industry Regulatory Authority governs securities arbitration. It is situated in the USA.

A range of conflicts, including those involving allegations of fraud, misrepresentation, unsuitability, and breach of fiduciary duty, are settled through securities arbitration. The arbitrators who hear the disputes are often skilled in securities law and arbitration, and it is frequently cheaper and faster than going to court.

When an investor submits a claim to FINRA, the securities arbitration procedure normally gets started. An arbitrator will be tasked with hearing both sides' arguments and rendering a decision on the claim. The arbitrator's ruling is typically enforceable and binding, and it may include a damages award or other types of remedies.

The fact that investors who have signed contracts with their brokerage firms that contain arbitration clauses are typically required to participate in securities arbitration is one of its distinctive characteristics. This suggests that investors might not be able to file legal claims and may be forced to settle their differences through the securities arbitration process.

A useful method for resolving conflicts between investors and their brokerage companies or financial advisors is securities arbitration. When investors have been affected by the activities of their financial advisors, it can help to ensure that they can collect damages or other types of relief through a relatively quick and efficient process.

Contractual provisions known as government-supported arbitration clauses compel disputes to be settled through arbitration rather than in court and are backed by the government. These provisions can be included in a range of agreements, including consumer contracts, business-to-business agreements, and employment contracts.

The U.S. government's passage of the Federal Arbitration Act (FAA) is one illustration of a government-backed arbitration clause. In 1925, Congress. According to the FAA, arbitration agreements are legitimate, enforceable, and irrevocable, and courts are required to uphold them in accordance with their terms. The U.S. has interpreted the FAA. Supreme Court to apply to a variety of contracts, including consumer and employment contracts.

The 2017 rule from the Consumer Financial Protection Bureau (CFPB) is another illustration of a government-backed arbitration clause. Financial institutions are not allowed to include forced arbitration clauses in consumer contracts for financial products including credit cards, auto loans, and other items under the CFPB rule. Also, the rule permits consumers to sue financial institutions collectively, something that was previously barred by many mandatory arbitration provisions.

Government-backed arbitration clauses can help parties to disputes in a number of ways. For instance, compared to going to court, arbitration can be quicker, less expensive, and more private. Yet, there are also worries that customers or employees may not have the same rights or safeguards in arbitration as they would in court, and that arbitration can be skewed in favor of businesses or employers.

Government-backed arbitration clauses can offer a practical method for resolving conflicts in a range of situations. When approving such clauses, it is crucial for parties to carefully weigh the advantages and disadvantages of arbitration and to make sure their rights and interests are effectively safeguarded during the arbitration process.

19.1. Enforcement of Arbitration Clauses

Contractual provisions known as arbitration clauses mandate that disputes be settled through arbitration rather than through the more conventional legal process of going to court. In the United States, the Federal Arbitration Act (FAA) typically governs the execution of arbitration provisions.

Courts must uphold arbitration agreements in accordance with the FAA unless there is a legitimate legal justification not to do so. Fraud, duress, or unconscionability are a few instances of acceptable legal defenses. Also, if the arbitration clause goes against public policy, it might not always be enforced.

The opposite party may bring a motion to compel arbitration in court if a party refuses to abide by an arbitration agreement. In the event that the arbitration agreement is upheld by the court, arbitration rather than litigation will be mandated for the parties.

It's crucial to remember that the way arbitration clauses are enforced can differ depending on the jurisdiction and the specifics of the arbitration agreement. It is always advised to speak with a lawyer who is knowledgeable about the laws in your country and the details of your particular contract.

19.2. The Validity of Arbitration Clauses is being tested.

It is necessary to determine if an arbitration clause is enforceable and binding in order to evaluate its legality. These are a few elements that could be taken into account while determining whether an arbitration clause is legitimate.

Agreement between parties. An arbitration clause must be accepted by both parties in order to be legally binding. This means that the clause must be stated in the contract in plain language and cannot be buried in the small print or a separate document. The conditions must have been reviewed and discussed by both parties.

Unconscionability. It might be impossible to enforce it if it is unconscionable. You cannot enforce it when it appears to be extremely biased or repressive since it is inherently highly unjust. Courts may take into account elements like the parties' bargaining power, the terms' clarity, and the arbitration fees.

Fraud or coercion. An arbitration clause may be void if it was agreed to fraudulently or under duress, such as when one party was coerced into signing the agreement.

A public policy. If an arbitration clause attempts to waive statutory rights or safeguards or otherwise violates public policy, it may be ruled unenforceable.

The clause's scope. The scope of the arbitration clause, including whether it applies to all parties and whether it covers the specific dispute in question, may also be taken into account by the court.

It can be difficult to determine whether an arbitration clause is valid, and it may be necessary to carefully examine the relevant facts and circumstances. To assess the legality of an arbitration clause, it is frequently advisable to speak with a lawyer with experience in arbitration law.

19.3. The modification of an Arbitration Clause

An arbitration clause may be modified, although doing so often needs consent from both parties. In order for a revision to an arbitration clause to be enforceable, it should generally be made in writing and signed by both parties.

It's crucial to remember that changing an arbitration clause after a dispute has developed can be more difficult. In such circumstances, the existing arbitration agreement may need to be modified or amended separately, and the parties may need to seek the arbitrator's or the court's consent.

It's crucial to take into account any applicable laws or regulations that might control the alteration of arbitration agreements. For instance, certain countries could demand that amendments be provided in a particular manner or might impose restrictions on the kinds of alterations that can be made to an arbitration agreement.

In order to make sure that a revision to an arbitration clause is valid and enforceable, it should be done carefully and with the help of legal counsel.

19.4. The right to arbitrate can be waived.

By doing acts that are inconsistent with the wish to arbitrate the issue, such as submitting a lawsuit in court, engaging in extensive discovery, or delaying the request for arbitration, a party may give up the right to arbitration.

In order to assess whether a party has waived the right to arbitrate, courts will often consider all of the relevant facts. The main issue is whether the party's actions have sufficiently violated the right to arbitrate, making it unfair or detrimental to let the party to alter course and request arbitration.

It's crucial to remember that, depending on the jurisdiction and the provisions of the arbitration agreement, there can be particular laws or rules that apply to a waiver of the right to arbitrate. For instance, certain arbitration agreements might have language addressing waiver, and some jurisdictions might demand a clear declaration of desire to forego arbitration.

In general, parties should exercise caution not to act in a manner inconsistent with their intention to arbitrate and should get legal advice to make sure that their conduct does not unintentionally amount to a waiver of their right to arbitrate a dispute.

The parties to the arbitration may be concerned about excessive arbitration fees. The majority of this is made up of administrative fees for the arbitration and arbitrator fees. These costs could make it difficult to participate in the arbitration process in some circumstances since they are so high.

These are some possible responses to exorbitant arbitration expenses.

The arbitration clause should be negotiated. The specifics of the arbitration clause, including the division of arbitration expenses, may be subject to negotiation between the parties. For instance, the parties may decide to equally divide the expense of arbitration or mandate that the losing party cover the costs.

A different arbitrator should be chosen. Other arbitrators could have different fee schedules and charge less. When choosing a supplier, parties may want to compare their fees.

Ask for fee reductions or waivers. For parties who can prove they have a financial necessity, certain arbitration services will waive or reduce their fees. Parties may want to learn more about these possibilities.

Think about alternate dispute-resolution procedures. Consider negotiation or mediation as alternatives to arbitration as they might be less expensive.

Challenge inflated costs. In rare circumstances, parties may be able to object to excessive arbitration fees as being against the law or unfair. To establish the best course of action, it may be necessary to speak with legal counsel as this can be a challenging and unpredictable tactic.

In general, parties to the arbitration may have serious concerns about exorbitant arbitration fees. It's crucial for parties to thoroughly analyze the arbitration clause's provisions and look for ways to lower or mitigate the arbitration fee.

Chapter 21. The Arbitration Tribunal.

A group of arbitrators chosen to settle a conflict between parties is known as an arbitration tribunal, sometimes known as an arbitral tribunal. It is a private venue for out-of-court conflict resolution, and its conclusions are usually conclusive on the parties.

Depending on the arbitration agreement or the regulations governing the arbitration processes, the number of arbitrators on a tribunal may vary. There are often one or three arbitrators. If there are three arbitrators, one arbitrator may be chosen by each party. The third arbitrator will then be selected by the first two arbitrators. If they believe it would be more beneficial, they may also decide to serve as the presiding arbitrator.

The tribunal's job is to hear the facts and arguments put out by the parties and render a judgment based on the case's merits. An arbitral award is what the tribunal issues; it is final, binds the parties, and can only be contested in certain situations, including when there is proof of fraud or misconduct.

Generally, the most significant part in the entire arbitration process is played by the arbitration tribunal. It is also in charge of making the crucial judgment call that will end the parties' conflict.

The following stages typically comprise the arbitral tribunal process.

Concession to Arbitration. By signing a contract with an arbitration clause, the parties' consent to subject their dispute to arbitration. The parameters of the arbitration are outlined in this clause, together with the procedures that will be followed and the number of arbitrators to be chosen.

Choose the arbitrators. In accordance with the rules of the arbitration agreement, the parties choose the arbitrator(s). If the parties are unable to come to an agreement on the arbitrator or arbitrators, the arbitrator will be appointed by the appointing authority specified in the arbitration agreement or by the applicable arbitration rules (s).

First Concerns. Following their appointment, the arbitrator(s) will hold a preliminary hearing to go over the arbitration's procedural details, including the timetable for the proceedings, the exchange of pleadings and evidence, and the language to be used.

Pleadings and evidence are exchanged. The claim and defense declarations, as well as any supporting documentation and proof, are exchanged in writing by the parties.

Hearing. Each party will make its case in front of the arbitrator(s), including oral arguments and witness testimonies.

Arbitral Decision. The arbitrator(s) will choose the format of an arbitral award after taking into account the arguments and evidence put forth by the parties. This decision is final and binding on the parties.

Enforcement. The parties are required to follow the conditions of the arbitral award once it is made. When the arbitration agreement calls for judicial enforcement or where the award must be upheld in a separate country, it may occasionally be essential to enforce the decision in court.

The arbitral tribunal process is generally intended to offer a fair and effective means of resolving disputes outside of court, with the parties having more influence over the procedure and results than in traditional litigation.

Chapter 23. The appointment process at the beginning of arbitration.

The following steps are commonly included in the appointment procedure that starts an arbitration.

Choosing an arbitrator. A single arbitrator or a panel of arbitrators who will preside over the arbitration must be chosen by the parties to the dispute. If the parties are unable to agree on an arbitrator, they may request a list of suitable arbitrators from a third-party body, such as the American Arbitration Association or the International Chamber of Commerce.

Communication of Information. Once an arbitrator has been chosen, the parties are required to reveal any material that may affect the arbitrator's objectivity or independence. For instance, the opposite party must be informed if the arbitrator has a financial interest in one of the parties.

Selecting the arbitrator. Following the exchange of information, the parties must affirm the choice of the arbitrator by signing a document that outlines the arbitration's parameters and the arbiter's authority.

Conference in advance. The parties may participate in a preliminary meeting with the arbitrator to go over the arbitration's procedural details, including the venue for hearings, how to submit evidence, and when the arbitration will take place.

In general, a fair and effective arbitration proceeding is dependent on the appointment procedure that takes place before the start of the arbitration. The arbitrator must be chosen by the agreement of the parties, who must also set the arbitration's procedural rules and reveal any material that could jeopardize the arbiter's independence or impartiality.

Chapter 24. Arbitration Umpire or Chairperson.

A chairperson or umpire may preside over the arbitration proceedings in some forms of arbitration, especially those involving a panel of arbitrators.

The umpire or chairperson is frequently a seasoned arbitrator or legal expert and is typically chosen by the parties or by the other arbitrators on the panel. The chairperson's or umpire's job is to oversee the arbitration hearings. The umpire or chairperson is in charge of running the arbitration sessions, making decisions about procedural issues, and overseeing the smooth and impartial operation of the arbitration.

Control the arbitrators' panel. If a panel of arbitrators is involved in the arbitration, the umpire or chairperson is in charge of directing the proceedings and seeing that the panel agrees on any necessary judgments.

Make a final choice. If the panel of arbitrators is unable to come to an agreement, the umpire or chairperson may in some situations be required to make the final decision in the arbitration.

Ultimately, the chairperson's or umpire's job in arbitration is crucial to making sure that the proceeding is fair and effective and that the parties obtain a conclusion that is well-supported and well-reasoned.

The person who presides over the arbitration proceedings is sometimes referred to as the "umpire" or "chairperson" in arbitration. The two jobs do, however, differ in a few minor ways.

Umpire. In a three-member arbitration panel, where two of the arbitrators are chosen by each party, an umpire is often appointed. In the event that the other two arbitrators are unable to agree on a resolution, the umpire's job is to serve as a tie-breaker. In other words, the umpire only participates in the arbitration if there is a tie between the other two arbitrators on a particular point.

Chairperson. A chairperson is often chosen to preside over the arbitration proceedings and oversee the panel in an arbitration panel of one to three members. The chairperson may also be charged with extra duties, such as giving the arbitration's final judgment or issuing procedural orders.

Therefore, even though the terms "umpire" and "chairperson" are frequently used interchangeably, the main distinction is that an umpire only participates in the arbitration when the other arbitrators are at a standstill, whereas a chairperson is always present and has more authority over how the arbitration is conducted.

Chapter 25. The role of the Arbitrator Advocate.

Advocates for arbitrators are experts who focus on defending clients in arbitration procedures. They frequently have backgrounds in law or conflict resolution and are knowledgeable about the arbitration procedure as well as the pertinent laws and rules.

Client representation and case presentation before the arbitrator or arbitration panel are part of their duties. They might assist clients with case preparation, evidence gathering, and the drafting of court papers like pleadings and briefs. Additionally, they could offer direction and counsel regarding the legal and tactical facets of the case and engage in settlement or other dispute resolution negotiations with the other party.

Arbitrator advocates may operate as independent consultants, attorneys for corporations, or law firms. They might also be experts in particular fields of law or industries, like building, trading abroad, or intellectual property.

In general, arbitrator advocates are crucial in making sure that their client's interests are adequately protected during the arbitration process and that they have the best opportunity of coming out on top.

Depending on the situation, an arbitrator may be dismissed in a variety of ways. Here are a few such scenarios where an arbitrator might be fired.

Voluntary departure. Due to unrecognized conflicts of interest or for personal reasons, an arbitrator may decide to voluntarily leave the case.

Mutual consent. The arbitrator may be dismissed and a new one chosen with the consent of both parties to the dispute.

If a party feels that the arbitrator is biased or has a conflict of interest, they may raise a challenge. The challenge must be supported by specific arguments, and the opposing side must offer proof of their assertion. The challenge is typically heard by a court or an impartial agency.

Violation of the arbitration's rules. A party may request the dismissal of an arbitrator if they do not follow the arbitration rules or operate outside of their authority.

A court case. In some situations, a party may try to have an arbitrator dismissed by bringing a lawsuit in court.

Depending on the arbitration agreement or the relevant law, there may be a difference in the procedure for dismissing an arbitrator. To fully grasp your options and legal rights in the event that you must have an arbitrator removed, it is crucial to speak with a knowledgeable arbitration attorney.

26.1. The Resignation of the Arbitrator

Resigning from a case as an arbitrator can delay and disrupt the arbitration process. An arbitrator may quit for a number of reasons, including illness, a conflict of interest, or personal considerations.

In this case, if there is more than one arbitrator, the parties may need to appoint a new arbitrator or proceed with the current arbitrators. The arbitration agreement and relevant law will determine the procedure for choosing a new arbitrator.

The parties shall abide by the procedure for selecting arbitrators that have been agreed upon by the parties. They might have to abide by the arbitration institution's guidelines or the relevant law if there is no established procedure.

In rare circumstances, an arbitrator's retirement can constitute a breach of the arbitration agreement or contract, in which case the party who was wronged might be entitled to damages or other relief. To comprehend your alternatives in this circumstance, it is crucial to carefully analyze the contents of the arbitration agreement and speak with an arbitration lawyer with experience.

The scenario surrounding an arbitrator's departure can be difficult for the parties concerned, but with the right coordination, cooperation, and advice from legal professionals, they can come up with a solution that best suits their needs.

26.2. The Death of the Arbitrator.

An arbitrator's passing is a rare but potential occurrence that might impede arbitration and add time to the process. To continue the arbitration process in such a case, the parties might need to choose a new arbiter.

The parties must nominate a new arbitrator or, if there are more than one, proceed with the remaining arbitrators if the arbitrator passes away before rendering an award. The arbitration agreement and relevant law will determine the procedure for choosing a new arbitrator.

The parties shall abide by the procedure for selecting arbitrators that has been agreed upon by the parties. They might have to abide by the arbitration institution's guidelines or the relevant law if there is no established procedure.

If the arbitrator has previously informed the parties of the award after making it but before issuing it, the ruling may still be enforceable. The parties will need to select a new arbitrator to issue a new award if the award has not been conveyed.

The award will remain valid even if the arbitrator passes away after issuing it unless it is contested on the grounds of the arbitrator's passing. The award may need to be reviewed or a new one made in this situation, therefore the parties may need to choose a new arbitrator.

In any event, the loss of an arbitrator can present difficult circumstances for the parties, but with effective coordination, cooperation, and advice from legal professionals, they can come up with a solution that best meets their needs.

26.3. Appointing a New Arbitrator after the Resignation or Death of the Previous One. The parties might need to choose a new arbitrator to carry on the arbitration proceedings if an arbitrator steps down or passes away. The arbitration agreement and relevant law will determine the procedure for choosing a new arbitrator.

The parties shall abide by the procedure for selecting arbitrators that has been agreed upon by the parties. They might have to abide by the arbitration institution's guidelines or the relevant law if there is no established procedure.

Upon the resignation or passing of the former arbitrator, the following are some general steps to take.

The parties must inform one another, as well as any applicable arbitration institution, of the arbitrator's resignation or death.

The arbitration agreement is being reviewed. The procedure for choosing a new arbitrator should be outlined in the arbitration agreement, which the parties should check.

Choosing a new arbitrator. The process for selecting a new arbitrator must be followed, or the parties must come to an agreement on one. They could have to seek the arbitration organization or the court to appoint a new arbitrator if they are unable to come to an agreement.

Information and Verification. Both parties must agree on the new arbiter, who must disclose any potential conflicts of interest.

Progress of the proceedings. The arbitration proceedings may proceed after a new arbitrator has been chosen and confirmed.

If you need to select a new arbitrator due to the resignation or demise of the current one, it is crucial to speak with an experienced arbitration lawyer to understand your options and rights. Overall, the process of selecting a new arbitrator may take longer and cost more money, but it is crucial to make sure that the arbitration is neutral, impartial, and successful.

26.4. The Arbitrator Has Immunity from Being Sued.

Arbitrators frequently enjoy some kind of immunity or protection from being sued or held accountable for their actions while carrying out their duties in many jurisdictions. This immunity is meant to encourage arbitrators to render fair and impartial judgments without concern for reprisals or legal action.

Depending on the jurisdiction and the particular facts of the case, the immunity's reach can change. In general, arbitrators may be exempt from liability for actions or inactions taken in the course of their responsibilities and with due care. This covers judgments rendered throughout the arbitration process, such as evidence decisions, procedural judgments, and the determination on the merits.

This immunity is not unqualified, and it may be subject to some restrictions and exceptions. An arbitrator might be held accountable, for instance, if they go beyond the bounds of their authority or exhibit dishonest or illegal behavior.

In specific situations, such as when the arbitrator participates in misconduct or transgresses ethical standards, the immunity of an arbitrator may also be waived by agreement between the parties.

Generally, although not completely, an arbitrator's immunity from lawsuits can offer some degree of legal defense. To reduce the possibility of legal action, arbitrators must act in good faith, within the scope of their powers and responsibilities, and in accordance with ethical norms. In order to fully understand their rights and alternatives in the event that they think an arbitrator has acted incorrectly or illegally, parties should also speak with an experienced arbitration attorney.

26.5. The Jurisdiction of the Arbitral Tribunal.

The ability of an arbitral tribunal to hear and resolve a specific issue is referred to as its jurisdiction. This power stems from the parties' agreement to have their disagreement arbitrated.

Since arbitration is a consensual process, the parties must have consented to have their dispute arbitrated in the first place. A contract, a separate arbitration agreement, or the actions of the parties themselves may contain or imply an arbitration clause.

The parties must also agree on the tribunal's jurisdictional authority once they have agreed to arbitrate a dispute. This could entail deciding on the particular problems that will be addressed by the tribunal, the rules and procedures that will be used for the arbitration, and the terminology that will be used during the arbitration.

The governing law may also place restrictions on the arbitral tribunal's authority by mandating that some conflicts go before a court or limiting the kinds of disputes that can be arbitrated.

As long as the disagreement is covered by the arbitration agreement and is not illegal, the arbitral tribunal generally has jurisdiction over any dispute that the parties have agreed to arbitrate.

The tribunal may be obliged to establish its jurisdiction as a preliminary issue if there is a disagreement regarding it. Depending on the arbitration rules and the relevant law, a party may contest this decision or request that a court review it.

Overall, the jurisdiction of the arbitral tribunal defines the extent of the tribunal's authority to decide the dispute and the enforcement of its judgment, making it a crucial component of the arbitration process.

26.6. The Arbitral Hearing Proceedings.

The hearings that take place during arbitration in which the parties and the arbitrator(s) present evidence, make arguments, and reach a decision are known as arbitral hearing processes. Depending on the arbitration agreement, the applicable law, and the norms of the arbitral institution, the steps for an arbitral hearing may differ, although they generally follow a similar pattern.

Pre-hearing discussion. The arbitrator(s) may meet with the parties before the arbitration hearing to go over the specifics of the arbitration process, including the scope of the dispute, the types of evidence that will be used, and any other potential concerns.

Beginning remarks. At the start of the hearing, the parties may give opening remarks explaining their positions on the dispute and the evidence they plan to submit.

Demonstration of the facts. To bolster their arguments, the parties may offer documentation, witness testimony, or expert opinions. The arbitrator(s) may make inquiries and ask for more information or evidence.

Cross-examination. After a witness has given testimony, the opposing side may have the chance to cross-examine the witness in order to question their credibility or learn more.

Concluding points. The parties may make closing arguments at the conclusion of the hearing to restate their case and encourage the arbitrator(s) to find in their favor.

Decision. The arbitrator(s) will issue a binding decision on the dispute after taking into account the arguments and facts put forth.

The arbitrator(s) may also render procedural decisions throughout the hearing, such as admitting or rejecting evidence, settling conflicts between the parties, and deciding the sequence of presentations. During the hearing, the parties may also have the chance to ask for a break or an adjournment.

Generally, the arbitral hearing proceedings give the parties a stage to argue their case and gain a definitive resolution to the conflict.

26.7. Duties of the Arbitral Tribunal.

The obligations of an arbitral tribunal may differ based on the particular arbitration procedure and relevant laws, but generally speaking, they include;

Determining its legal authority. The tribunal must first decide if it is qualified to hear the particular case.

Taking charge of the proceedings. The tribunal is in charge of efficiently and fairly executing the arbitration proceedings.

Imposing rules of procedure. Orders for the arbitration's conduct, such as submission deadlines for evidence or briefing, may be made by the tribunal.

Implementing the law. The tribunal must decide the case based on the appropriate legislation after applying it to the disagreement.

Assessing the information. To reach a conclusion, the tribunal must consider the evidence that the parties have submitted.

Giving out a verdict. The disagreement must be settled by a final award from the tribunal.

Managing spending. The tribunal may be in charge of overseeing the arbitration's costs, including the arbitrator's fees and expenses as well as the administrative costs associated with the arbitration.

Keeping things private. The tribunal is obligated to keep the arbitration proceedings and any information shared in private.

Upholding moral principles. Throughout the arbitration procedure, the tribunal must uphold moral principles and behave impartially and independently.

Ultimately, the tribunal's main responsibility is to settle the issue in a fair and unbiased manner in accordance with the law that applies and the conditions of the parties' agreement.

26.8. The Procedure for the Arbitration Session.

In the arbitration procedure, a neutral third party, sometimes referred to as an arbitrator or an arbitral tribunal, is used to render a legally enforceable ruling about the dispute. The following steps are frequently included in the arbitration process.

Starting the arbitration process. One party sends the other party a notice of arbitration to begin the arbitration procedure. A summary of the dispute, the requested relief, and the arbitrator's name or the procedure for choosing an arbitrator are often included in this notice.

The selection of the arbiter. To settle the issue, the parties may decide on a single arbitrator or a panel of arbitrators. If the parties are unable to reach an agreement, the arbitrator will be chosen by the authority specified in the arbitration agreement or by applicable legislation (s).

A preliminary meeting. To consider procedural issues such the exchange of pleadings, discovery, and the timetable for the arbitration procedure, the arbitrator(s) may hold a preliminary conference.

Furnishing of proof. The parties provide the arbitrator(s) with evidence, which may include witness testimony, expert opinions, and written records.

Hearing. The arbitrator(s) hold a hearing during which the parties argue their cases and offer any supporting documentation. The hearing can take place in person or online.

Deliberation. The arbitrator(s) will think about their decision after the hearing and reach one. The judgment usually takes the form of a legally binding written award.

Enforcement. If the losing party does not voluntarily comply, the winning party may enforce the award in court.

Method of providing (and disputing) evidence. The method of submitting evidence, which may include written submissions, witness statements, or expert reports, may be agreed upon by the parties. The arbitrator(s) may also make a decision regarding arguments against the admissibility of evidence.

The hearing's location and time. The location and time of the hearing may be decided upon by the parties. If they can't come to an agreement, the arbitrator(s) will choose the day and location.

Translations and language. The language to be used in the arbitration procedures may be decided by the parties. If they are unable to reach a consensus, the arbitrator(s) will choose the language. There may also be a need for translation services.

Document and other evidence disclosure. It may be necessary for the parties to exchange essential documents and other proof with one another and the arbitrator (s).

Using interrogatories and/or pleas. It may be necessary for the parties to submit written pleadings or answer questions in order to set forth their viewpoints and provide more details.

Using legal counsel. Legal counsel may represent the parties and take part in the arbitration process.

Appointment of assessors and specialists. To offer guidance or help with the appraisal of the evidence, the parties or the arbitrator(s) may choose to hire experts or assessors.

Overall, taking care of these procedural issues permits the parties to submit their arguments and supporting evidence while also ensuring that the arbitration proceedings are fair and effective.

26.9. It is possible to appeal against an Award that was given by the Arbitral Tribunal. In general, there are few opportunities to contest an arbitral tribunal's decision. This is so that the disagreement can be resolved definitively and legally binding through arbitration. Yet, based on the current laws and regulations, it may occasionally be permissible to contest or appeal an award.

Depending on the jurisdiction and the relevant legislation, there may be a variety of grounds for contesting or appealing an award, but these usually include.

Absence of authority. The award may be contested if the arbitrator(s) went beyond their power or went beyond what was required of them.

Irregularities in the process. The award may be contested if there were significant procedural anomalies that compromised the fairness or integrity of the proceedings, including a breach of due process.

A public policy. The award may be contested if it contravenes fundamental principles of public policy, such as human rights, environmental preservation, or anti-corruption laws.

Factual or legal mistakes. The award may be contested if the arbitrator(s) made a legal or factual error that had an impact on how the dispute was resolved.

The particular legal justifications for contesting or appealing an award will be determined by the laws and regulations that apply. It is also crucial to keep in mind that there are typically only a few valid grounds for challenge or appeal, and that courts will typically respect the arbitrator's judgment.

In general, before agreeing to an arbitration agreement, parties should carefully analyze the applicable laws and procedures and be aware that the ruling may be final and enforceable.

26.10. Specialized Arbitration Organizations.

Services for conflict resolution are offered in a wide range of industries and sectors by numerous specialized arbitration organizations. Among the most well-known businesses are.

International Chamber of Commerce (ICC): The ICC is one of the top arbitration organizations in the world and offers services for resolving commercial disputes on an international scale.

American Arbitration Association (AAA): The AAA offers arbitration and mediation services for a range of conflicts, such as those involving business, construction, employment, and consumers.

An institution that specializes in resolving disputes between foreign investors and host nations is called the International Centre for Settlement of Investment Disputes (ICSID).

The LCIA, a prestigious international arbitration agency with its headquarters in London, offers conflict resolution services for business and investment issues.

Singapore International Arbitration Centre (SIAC): The SIAC is a preeminent Asian arbitration institution that offers services for resolving disputes involving transnational business transactions.

World Intellectual Property Organization (WIPO): The WIPO offers services for resolving disputes involving intellectual property, such as patents, trademarks, and copyrights.

A well-known nonprofit organization called the International Institute for Conflict Prevention and Resolution (CPR) offers dispute resolution services to a variety of industries, including healthcare, energy, and construction.

These organizations offer a neutral and effective platform for parties to settle their issues outside of the conventional judicial system and have established rules and processes for doing so.

26.11. Fees and expenses of an Arbitral Tribunal

A variety of variables, including the complexity of the dispute, the number of arbitrators engaged, the venue of the arbitration, and the length of the proceedings, will affect the amount of money spent on an arbitral tribunal.

A few hundred dollars to several thousand dollars per hour, depending on their level of experience and competence, is what arbitrators normally charge for their time spent working on the case. The arbitration institution's administrative costs, including filing and case management fees, must also be covered by the parties.

The cost of the hearing location, the arbitrators' travel costs, and any fees for expert witnesses or interpreters are additional costs related to arbitration. The location and the nature of the dispute might have a big impact on these costs as well.

To put things in perspective, depending on the aforementioned variables, the costs and fees for a normal international arbitration can reach millions of dollars. Before choosing to pursue arbitration, the parties should carefully weigh these costs; they may also want to include them in their overall litigation plan and budget.

26.12. The American Arbitration Association, AAA and ADR (Alternative Dispute Resolution Services)

It's common to refer to the American Arbitration Association as the AAA. It's non-profit. It offers services for alternative conflict resolution. That includes mediation and arbitration for conflict management. Its main office is in New York City, where it was established in 1926.

The AAA offers a variety of services to people, companies, and organizations, among them.

Arbitration. The AAA provides a thorough collection of arbitration rules and processes that can be altered to suit the needs of the disputing parties. Instead of taking their case to court, parties might agree to have their disagreement arbitrated in a private, secret, and legally binding process called arbitration.

Mediation. The AAA additionally provides mediation services, a non-binding method of conflict resolution.

Other services for resolving disputes. At the start of a trial, the AAA also conducts an impartial evaluation. Both mini-trials and dispute settlement panels can be used.

The AAA has a panel of mediators and arbitrators with expertise in a variety of business sectors and legal disciplines. In addition, the organization offers materials for educators and training programs for mediators, arbitrators, and other dispute-resolution specialists.

The AAA is one of the biggest and most reputable providers of alternative dispute resolution in the world, and its services are frequently utilized in complicated business disputes, employment issues, and other serious legal problems.

26.13. The FMCS organization of the USA. The Federal Mediation and Conciliation Service.

In the private sector, this organization offers mediation and conflict resolution services for labor-management issues. It is a reputable government organization in the United States. It operates on its own.

The FMCS collaborates with both unions and businesses to assist in resolving grievances, labor-management disputes, and other concerns. To assist in avoiding problems altogether, the agency also offers training and advisory services.

Professional mediators and arbitrators with significant knowledge of labor-management relations work for the FMCS. These mediators and arbitrators collaborate with employers and unions to find areas of agreement, consider dispute resolution possibilities, and create solutions that are acceptable to all parties.

Both sides to a labor-management conflict may use the FMCS's voluntary and discreet services. The agency's objective is to assist parties in coming to an amicable resolution to their disagreement without the need for a strike or lockout.

The FMCS also offers mediation and conflict resolution services to the federal government, as well as to state and local governments, in addition to its work in the private sector. The organization has offices all around the country, and companies and unions from all spheres of society can use its services.

The FMCS was formed by the Taft-Hartley Act (Labor-Management Relations Act, published in 1947).

Chapter 27. International Arbitration.

When parties from different nations or legal systems disagree, international arbitration is a well-liked alternative dispute resolution technique that is used to resolve the conflict. An impartial arbitrator or a panel of arbitrators renders a final, enforceable ruling in this process, which is confidential, private, and binding.

International arbitration is frequently used to settle commercial disputes in cross-border transactions, giving the parties a neutral forum instead of resorting to the courts of one of their home nations. In international arbitration, arbitrators may be chosen from a variety of legal systems and nations and are typically chosen for their industry knowledge.

International conventions typically provide the rules and processes governing international arbitration. Many advantages of international arbitration include increased flexibility and control over the process, speedier conflict resolution than litigation, and the capacity to enforce verdicts internationally.

International arbitration may be pricey, too, and the arbitrators chosen and the arbitration procedures themselves have a big impact on how a dispute turns out. As a result, parties thinking about engaging in international arbitration should carefully assess their choices and consult with knowledgeable legal counsel.

Bypassing local judicial processes, parties can settle their issues through international arbitration in a private, secretive, and legally binding manner. This is especially helpful in cross-border transactions where the parties might choose a neutral forum rather than having to deal with the courts of one of the parties' home countries.

Chapter 28. International Bar Association and Arbitration.

In the area of international arbitration, the International Bar Association (IBA) has a considerable impact. It is a worldwide community of attorneys, law firms, and bar associations that offer a platform for legal experts to interact, share ideas, and advance best practices in international arbitration.

One of the IBA's busiest bodies, the Arbitration Committee is committed to advancing the use of arbitration as a method of settling international disputes. The group aims to create and promote arbitration standards, rules, and best practices as well as to give legal professionals opportunities for education and training.

In addition, the IBA sponsors a number of yearly events focused on international arbitration, such as the IBA Annual Conference, which features a number of lectures and workshops on the subject. Additionally, the IBA releases a number of publications, directives, and other materials pertaining to international arbitration that are well regarded and accepted by attorneys and arbitrators globally.

In conclusion, the IBA has made a substantial contribution to the growth and promotion of international arbitration and has been instrumental in developing best practices and standards for those working in this area.

Chapter 29. The History of International Arbitration

International arbitration has a long history that dates back to a time when conflicts between governments or between people were frequently settled by diplomatic negotiations or by the intervention of a third party. Nonetheless, the history of contemporary international arbitration dates back to the 19th century.

In the late 1860s, a dispute between the United States and Great Britain known as the Alabama Claims arbitration served as one of the early instances of contemporary international arbitration. Damages suffered by Confederate ships built in Britain during the American Civil War gave rise to the issue. A tribunal made up of five arbitrators—one each from the United States, Great Britain, and three other European nations—resolved the dispute.

In order to use arbitration to settle conflicts between governments, the Permanent Court of Arbitration (PCA) was founded in The Hague, Netherlands, in 1899. The PCA is the oldest international organization still in existence.

International arbitration gained prominence in the 20th century, particularly in the area of business disputes. Later came the New York-based Convention on the Recognition and Enforcement of International Arbitral Awards for the Business Community. It took place in 1958. It made using international arbitration as a viable choice for parties conducting cross-border business.

With several international conventions, institutions, and rules governing the procedure, international arbitration is now a generally acknowledged method of settling disputes between parties from other nations or legal systems.

Chapter 30. The Convention on the Recognition and Enforcement of Foreign Arbitral Awards; Enforcement of Arbitral Tribunal Awards in a Global Context.

The enforcement of arbitral tribunal decisions across borders is governed by the New York Convention. With very few exceptions, including lack of due process or public policy, arbitral awards may be accepted and upheld globally in accordance with the Agreement. To have an arbitral award enforced, a party often needs to make an application to the relevant country's competent court. The Agreement provides a reliable and effective means of resolving disputes by making it easier to enforce arbitral judgments abroad. The Convention, which has more than 160 signatories, has received widespread support from countries all around the world.

The parties may attempt to enforce an arbitral award in any other Convention country by delivering the award to the competent court along with evidence of the arbitration agreement and the award itself. The court may then decline to accept and uphold the judgment for a select few reasons, such as if the arbitration agreement was null and unlawful or the judgment was rendered in violation of the law.

The Convention has considerably facilitated international trade and investment by providing a stable and predictable framework for resolving disputes. While it has helped to promote arbitration as a preferred method of dispute resolution in business transactions, parties may be certain that their judgments will be upheld internationally.

Chapter 31. Interstate Arbitration.

The term "interstate arbitration" refers to the legal procedure known as arbitration used to settle disputes between two or more states.

Disputes between states over matters like territorial boundaries, water rights, environmental concerns, and commercial disputes are frequently settled by interstate arbitration. Interstate arbitration is often controlled by international law as well as any particular guidelines or processes that the parties have agreed upon.

Although the results of interstate arbitration can differ, they are normally enforceable and binding. This implies that the parties involved must abide by the arbitrator's ruling. The other party may utilize the courts or other legal mechanisms to enforce the agreement if one of the parties refuses to comply.

Chapter 32. Arbitration in England.

In England and Wales, arbitration is a prominent method for resolving disputes and is frequently used in civil cases involving business conflicts, disputes over construction projects, and other issues. The arbitration process in England and Wales is governed by the Arbitration Act 1996.

In England, arbitration is often handled by one arbitrator or a panel of arbitrators who are selected by the parties to the dispute. The arbitrator's decisions are final and enforceable in court, and they are frequently subject matter experts in dispute.

The fact that arbitration in England is frequently quicker and less formal than going to court is one of its benefits. The process is more in the hands of the parties, who can also pick the arbitrator, the venue, and the rules that will be followed. This can make it a more flexible and affordable choice than going to court.

Moreover, arbitration in England is confidential, so neither the specifics of the dispute nor the arbitrator's judgment are made public. For companies hoping to avoid bad press or reputational harm, this might be a crucial consideration.

Overall, arbitration is a well-recognized and successful method of resolving disputes in England, providing parties with a flexible and private alternative to courtroom action.

Chapter 33. The History of Arbitration in England.

In England, arbitration has a lengthy history that dates back to the Middle Ages, when tradesmen and merchants utilized it to settle disagreements over contracts and products. During time, arbitration grew in significance as a means of resolving disputes in England, where it was sanctioned by the legal system.

The Arbitration Act of 1698, which established a framework for the enforcement of arbitration agreements and verdicts, was one of the significant breakthroughs in the history of arbitration in England. This law contributed to the acceptance of arbitration as a valid and respected method of resolving disputes in England.

In England, arbitration grew in popularity as a litigation substitute in the 19th century, notably for business conflicts. As trade and business expanded as a result of the Industrial Revolution, so did the demand for effective and quick conflict-resolution procedures.

With the passage of the Arbitration Act of 1950 and the Arbitration Act of 1979, the law of arbitration in England underwent further alterations in the 20th century. The foundation for conducting arbitration hearings and enforcing arbitral rulings was expanded by this legislation.

The enactment of the Arbitration Act 1996, which revised and consolidated the law of arbitration in England and Wales, has been the most significant recent development. Due to the increasing significance of arbitration in global trade and business, this act modernized arbitration law and made it more approachable and flexible.

In England today, arbitration is a well-respected and well-established method of resolving a variety of civil and business issues. The long-standing significance of arbitration as a method of resolving disputes and its continual development and adaptation to shifting legal and commercial environments are both made clear by the history of arbitration in England.

Chapter 34. The London Court of International Arbitration.

Based in London, UK, it is. One of the most reputable and often used institutes for international arbitration, it was established in 1892.

The LCIA offers several different services in connection with international commercial arbitration, such as managing arbitrations, selecting arbitrators, and setting up hearing locations. The LCIA's rules are recognized as some of the most advanced and adaptable in the world, and many other arbitral institutions have adopted them and utilized them as a model for other international arbitration procedures.

Using the LCIA offers an impartial and unbiased platform for resolving disputes, which is one of its main benefits. Also, the LCIA has a solid reputation for professionalism and effectiveness, and courts all over the world generally respect and uphold its rulings.

The LCIA is renowned for its skill in arbitrating intricate and expensive commercial disputes, especially those involving money, energy, construction, and international trade. Its arbitrators frequently have a range of diverse legal and cultural backgrounds and are typically skilled and informed in these fields.

The court is a prestigious and dependable institution for international business arbitration, providing parties with a neutral and impartial forum for amicably and speedily resolving disagreements.

Chapter 35. International Chamber of Commerce.

With its headquarters in Paris, France, the International Chamber of Commerce (ICC) was established in 1919. With more than six million members from more than 130 nations, it is the biggest business association in the world.

The ICC offers a variety of services to firms all over the world and is crucial in fostering global trade and investment. Facilitating international arbitration through the ICC is one of its most crucial duties.

A renowned venue for the settlement of disputes involving transnational business is the ICC International Court of Arbitration. As one of the most reputable and effective arbitral institutions in the world, it offers a neutral and impartial platform for settling disputes between enterprises from various nations.

The ICC Court of Arbitration provides a variety of services in connection with international arbitration, such as managing arbitrations, selecting arbitrators, and setting up hearing locations. Additionally, it provides a variety of arbitration rules from which parties may select in accordance with their requirements and preferences.

The fact that the ICC Court of Arbitration offers a high degree of professionalism and expertise, with experienced arbitrators from a wide range of diverse legal and cultural backgrounds, is one of the main benefits of using it. In addition, the ICC offers a variety of additional services to businesses, such as policy lobbying, training in dispute settlement, and research and thought leadership.

Overall, the ICC is a successful organization for promoting global trade and investment and offering companies a fair and impartial platform for dispute resolution.

Chapter 36. ICC Commercial Crime Services (CCS)

Businesses can take advantage of a number of services provided by the CCS, such as training and education programs, risk management tools and services, and information and intelligence on fraud and commercial crime. Based in London, UK, it is.

Also, it runs a number of specialist divisions, such as the Financial Investigation Bureau, which offers corporations and law enforcement organizations financial investigation services.

The CCS is in charge of the International Maritime Bureau. It examines data pertaining to ships that have been the targets of piracy and other crimes. When ships are being taken advantage of by pirates, they also alert authorities all around the world.

The CCS also manages the FraudNet network, a worldwide association of attorneys with expertise in fraud prevention and asset recovery. Members of FraudNet collaborate to assist businesses in regaining assets that have been misappropriated through fraud or other commercial crimes.

Overall, the ICC Commercial Crime Services contributes significantly to the advancement of moral and legal business conduct as well as the fight against fraud and commercial crime. Businesses all around the world frequently employ its services, and it has a solid reputation for professionalism and efficiency in resolving these challenges.

Promoting effective intellectual property (IP) protection and enforcement globally is BASCAP's main objective.

BASCAP collaborates with governments, politicians, and other stakeholders to create and put into action policies that deal with the underlying issues that lead to piracy and counterfeiting. In order to promote best practices and offer training and capacity-building initiatives, the organization collaborates closely with companies, industry groups, and other organizations.

BASCAP engages in a variety of important tasks.

Raising awareness and advocating. BASCAP seeks to increase public understanding of the harm that piracy and counterfeiting do to economies, consumers, and enterprises. The group works with governments to strengthen IP laws and enforcement practices, among other advocacy initiatives.

Education and growth of capacity. To help organizations, decision-makers, and law enforcement agencies better grasp the risks and difficulties associated with piracy and counterfeiting, BASCAP offers training and educational programs.

Data gathering and analysis. BASCAP undertakes research and data analysis to learn more about the extent and effects of piracy and counterfeiting. The organization makes use of this data to create strategies and policies that are supported by data.

Partnership formation. BASCAP strives to create alliances between organizations, corporations, and other stakeholders to support effective IP enforcement and protection.

In conclusion, BASCAP is an international organization that supports effective IP enforcement and protection all around the world.

Chapter 38. Business Action to Support the Information Society.

Businesses can more easily engage in the development and implementation of laws and activities relevant to the information society thanks to this organization, also known as BASIS.

BASIS collaborates with lawmakers, business associations, and other stakeholders to advance legislation and regulations that support innovation and the use of ICTs. The group works to support ICT use for sustainable development and to create an environment that is conducive to ICT industry enterprise.

The projects that BASIS is most focused on are listed below.

Policy development and advocacy. BASIS takes part in advocacy campaigns in favor of policies that promote the development and application of ICTs. The group attempts to make it simpler for companies to take part in developing information society-related policy frameworks.

Capacity development and training. BASIS provides training and capacity-building programs to assist businesses, governments, and other stakeholders in better understanding the potential of ICTs and encouraging their effective use for economic and social development.

Creation of a partnership. BASIS works to forge alliances between businesses, governments, and other stakeholders in order to advance the development and use of ICTs. The organization takes part in public-private partnerships to promote innovation and assist with the implementation of ICT initiatives.

Study and analysis. BASIS conducts research and data analysis to better understand the potential of ICTs for economic and social development. The organization uses this information to develop data-supported initiatives and policies.

BASIS is, in conclusion, a global organization for economic development. The group participates in advocacy activities, provides capacity-building and training programs, forges collaborations, conducts research and analyzes data in order to aid in the adoption of ICTs.

The NAA governs labor arbitrators in both Canada and the United States. It was established in 1947 and has since risen to the top of its field in North America.

Promoting arbitration as a practical means of resolving labor disputes is the NAA's main goal. Its members are renowned experts in labor arbitration who have years of experience as arbitrators. They are chosen to settle conflicts involving unions or other employee representatives and employers.

The NAA offers education and training to its members and other people who are interested in arbitration. It organizes annual conferences, seminars, and workshops that address a variety of labor arbitration-related subjects, including interest arbitration, grievance handling, contract administration, collective bargaining, and grievance handling.

The NAA supports academic inquiry into arbitration as well. It publishes a quarterly publication called The Labor Arbitration Yearbook that includes summaries of recent arbitration rulings as well as articles on hot themes in labor arbitration. The NAA additionally produces books and other information about arbitration.

The NAA is dedicated to elevating professionalism and moral behavior in the arbitration industry. Its members are bound by an ethics code that calls on them to act impartially, fairly, and honorably in all of their arbitrator-related interactions. Its goals are to advance the use of arbitration as a successful mechanism for resolving labor disputes, to educate and teach those who are interested in arbitration, to support research and scholarship in the area, and to advance professionalism and ethical behavior in the arbitration community.

Chapter 40. Arbitration in Europe.

In Europe, arbitration is a well-known kind of alternative conflict settlement. Instead of going to court, it is frequently employed in commercial and investment conflicts. National laws and international agreements regulate arbitration in Europe.

The legislative basis for arbitration has also been developed by the European Union (EU). A standard legal foundation for arbitration proceedings inside the EU is provided by the EU Arbitration Directive. The regulation lays out guidelines for national court jurisdiction and arbitration party rights.

Arbitration is usually regarded as a flexible, private, and efficient method of resolving disputes throughout Europe. Because it gives parties the option to pick their arbitrators, the arbitration's language and location, as well as the procedures to be followed, it is frequently chosen to litigation. In addition to being typically enforceable under international treaties, arbitration decisions are also easier to enforce than court judgements.

Arbitration does face certain difficulties in Europe, though. Making sure arbitrators are unbiased and independent is one of the biggest concerns. Some detractors contend that arbitrators might be biased or prone to conflicts of interest, undermining the impartiality and integrity of the arbitration process. The expense and duration of arbitration as well as the disparity in arbitration laws among European countries are further difficulties.

In conclusion, arbitration is a popular form of alternative dispute resolution in Europe and is governed by both domestic law and international agreements. There are numerous reputable arbitral institutions in Europe, and the EU has evolved its own legal framework for arbitration. Although though arbitration is typically seen as a flexible and successful method of settling conflicts, there are several issues that must be resolved in order to guarantee the fairness and credibility of the arbitration process.

In Germany, arbitration is a recognized alternative dispute settlement process. It is frequently employed in commercial and financial disputes where the parties concur that arbitration is preferable to litigation. The German Arbitration Act, often known as the DIS or Deutsche Institution für Schiedsgerichtsbarkeit, governs arbitration in Germany.

Germany's arbitrations are managed and supervised by the DIS, a self-regulatory agency. It lays forth procedures for holding arbitrations, such as guidelines for the selection and qualifications of arbitrators, how hearings should be conducted, and how arbitral rulings should be enforced. The DIS also supports in the selection of arbitrators by maintaining a list of qualified arbitrators.

Due to the parties' ability to select their arbitrators, the arbitration's language and location, as well as the procedures to be followed, arbitration is frequently favored to litigation in Germany. In addition to being typically enforceable under international treaties, arbitration decisions are also easier to enforce than court judgements.

The fact that arbitration in Germany is typically less formal and more flexible than judicial proceedings is one of its main benefits. As a result, disputes may be resolved more quickly and affordably. In cases when confidentiality is crucial, the confidentiality of arbitration proceedings might be a significant consideration.

Arbitration in Germany, like other jurisdictions, is not without difficulties. Making sure arbitrators are unbiased and independent is one of the biggest concerns. Conflicts of interest are strictly regulated by the DIS, and arbitrators are required to declare any potential conflicts before accepting an assignment. The expense and duration of arbitration as well as the disparity in arbitration laws among various jurisdictions are further difficulties.

In conclusion, the German Arbitration Act governs arbitration, a recognized alternative dispute settlement process in Germany (DIS). The DIS keeps a registry of accredited arbitrators and offers guidelines for conducting arbitrations. Arbitration in Germany typically offers benefits like confidentiality and award enforcement while being less formal and more flexible than judicial processes. To guarantee the impartiality and legitimacy of the arbitration procedure, various issues must be resolved.

In France, arbitration is a recognized form of alternative conflict settlement. It is frequently employed in commercial and financial disputes where the parties concur that arbitration is preferable to litigation. The French Code of Civil Procedure is the legal framework in France for arbitration.

Arbitrations in France are administered and supervised by the AFA, a self-regulatory agency. It lays forth procedures for holding arbitrations, such as guidelines for the selection and qualifications of arbitrators, how hearings should be conducted, and how arbitral rulings should be enforced. The AFA also aids in the selection of arbitrators by maintaining a list of qualified arbitrators.

Because the parties can pick their arbitrators, the arbitration's language and location, as well as the procedures to be followed, arbitration in France is frequently preferred to litigation. In addition to being typically enforceable under international treaties, arbitration decisions are also easier to enforce than court judgements.

The French Arbitration Association is based in France. The Association Française d'Arbitrage, or AFA, is how it is known in French. Arbitration in France is governed by this organization.

The fact that arbitration in France is typically less formal and more flexible than judicial proceedings is one of its main benefits. As a result, disputes may be resolved more quickly and affordably. In cases when confidentiality is crucial, the confidentiality of arbitration proceedings might be a significant consideration.

Arbitration in France does have its difficulties, just like in other countries. Making sure arbitrators are unbiased and independent is one of the biggest concerns. Conflicts of interest are strictly regulated by the AFA, and arbitrators are required to declare any potential conflicts before accepting an assignment. The expense and duration of arbitration as well as the disparity in arbitration laws among various jurisdictions are further difficulties.

In conclusion, the French Code of Civil Process and the French Arbitration Association control arbitration, a recognized alternative dispute settlement process (AFA). The AFA keeps a list of accredited arbitrators and offers guidelines for conducting arbitrations. Arbitration in France typically offers benefits like confidentiality and award enforcement while being less formal and more flexible than judicial processes. To guarantee the impartiality and legitimacy of the arbitration procedure, various issues must be resolved.

Chapter 43. Arbitration in Italy.

In Italy, arbitration is a recognized alternative dispute settlement process. It is frequently employed in commercial and financial disputes where the parties concur that arbitration is preferable to litigation. The Milan Chamber of Arbitration and the Italian Civil Process Code govern arbitration in Italy.

The self-regulatory authority that manages and oversees arbitrations in Italy is the Milan Chamber of Arbitration. It lays forth procedures for holding arbitrations, such as guidelines for the selection and qualifications of arbitrators, how hearings should be conducted, and how arbitral rulings should be enforced. The Chamber also aids in the selection of arbitrators by maintaining a list of qualified arbitrators.

Due to the parties' ability to select their arbitrators, the arbitration's language, location, and processes, arbitration is frequently chosen in Italy over litigation. In addition to being typically enforceable under international treaties, arbitration decisions are also easier to enforce than court judgements.

The fact that arbitration in Italy is typically less formal and more flexible than judicial processes is one of its main benefits. As a result, disputes may be resolved more quickly and affordably. In cases when confidentiality is crucial, the confidentiality of arbitration proceedings might be a significant consideration.

Arbitration in Italy does have its difficulties, just like in other jurisdictions. Making sure arbitrators are unbiased and independent is one of the biggest concerns. Conflicts of interest are strictly regulated by the Milan Chamber of Arbitration, and arbitrators are required to disclose any potential conflicts before accepting an appointment. The expense and duration of arbitration as well as the disparity in arbitration laws among various jurisdictions are further difficulties.

In conclusion, arbitration is a recognized alternative dispute resolution process in Italy, controlled by the Milan Chamber of Arbitration and the Italian Civil Process Code. The Chamber maintains a registry of accredited arbitrators and offers guidelines for conducting arbitrations. In Italy, arbitration often offers advantages like confidentiality and award enforcement while being less formal and more flexible than court processes. To guarantee the impartiality and legitimacy of the arbitration procedure, various issues must be resolved.

In Spain, arbitration is a recognized alternative dispute settlement process. It is frequently employed in commercial and financial disputes where the parties concur that arbitration is preferable to litigation. The Spanish Arbitration Act is the governing law for arbitration in Spain.

The CEA, a self-regulatory organization, is in charge of managing and monitoring arbitrations in Spain. It lays forth procedures for holding arbitrations, such as guidelines for the selection and qualifications of arbitrators, how hearings should be conducted, and how arbitral rulings should be enforced. The CEA also supports in the selection of arbitrators by maintaining a list of qualified arbitrators.

Because it gives parties the option to select their arbitrators, the arbitration's language and location, as well as the procedures to be followed, arbitration is frequently preferred to litigation in Spain. In addition to being typically enforceable under international treaties, arbitration decisions are also easier to enforce than court judgments.

The fact that arbitration in Spain is typically less formal and more flexible than judicial processes is one of its main benefits. As a result, disputes may be resolved more quickly and affordably. In cases when confidentiality is crucial, the confidentiality of arbitration proceedings might be a significant consideration.

Arbitration in Spain, like other jurisdictions, is not without difficulties. Making sure arbitrators are unbiased and independent is one of the biggest concerns. Conflicts of interest are strictly regulated by the CEA, and arbitrators are required to declare any potential conflicts before accepting an appointment. The expense and duration of arbitration as well as the disparity in arbitration laws among various jurisdictions are further difficulties.

In conclusion, arbitration is a recognized form of alternative dispute resolution in Spain. Arbitration is governed by the Spanish Arbitration Act and the Spanish Arbitration Club (CEA). The CEA keeps a list of accredited arbitrators and offers guidelines for conducting arbitrations. In Spain, arbitration hearings are typically less formal and more flexible than court proceedings and have benefits including confidentiality and award enforcement. To guarantee the impartiality and legitimacy of the arbitration procedure, various issues must be resolved.

Chapter 45. Arbitration in Portugal.

In Portugal, arbitration is a recognized alternative dispute settlement process. It is frequently employed in commercial and financial disputes where the parties concur that arbitration is preferable to litigation. The Portuguese Arbitration Act and the Portuguese Commercial Arbitration Center regulate arbitration in Portugal (Centro de Arbitragem Commercial or CAC).

Arbitrations in Portugal are administered and supervised by the CAC, a self-regulatory agency. It lays forth procedures for holding arbitrations, such as guidelines for the selection and qualifications of arbitrators, how hearings should be conducted, and how arbitral rulings should be enforced. The CAC also aids in the selection of arbitrators by maintaining a list of qualified arbitrators.

Because it gives parties the option to select their arbitrators, the arbitration's language, location, and processes, arbitration is frequently favored in Portugal to litigation. In addition to being typically enforceable under international treaties, arbitration decisions are also easier to enforce than court judgements.

The fact that arbitration in Portugal is typically less formal and more flexible than judicial processes is one of its main benefits. As a result, disputes may be resolved more quickly and affordably. In cases when confidentiality is crucial, the confidentiality of arbitration proceedings might be a significant consideration.

Arbitration in Portugal does have its difficulties, just like in other countries. Making sure arbitrators are unbiased and independent is one of the biggest concerns. Conflicts of interest are strictly regulated by the CAC, and arbitrators are required to declare any potential conflicts before accepting an appointment. The expense and duration of arbitration as well as the disparity in arbitration laws among various jurisdictions are further difficulties.

In conclusion, Portugal has a long history of using arbitration as a form of alternative conflict resolution, which is overseen by the Portuguese Arbitration

Act and the Portuguese Commercial Arbitration Centre (CAC). The CAC keeps a list of accredited arbitrators and offers guidelines for conducting arbitrations. In Portugal, arbitration hearings tend to be less formal and more flexible than court proceedings and include benefits like confidentiality and award enforcement. To guarantee the impartiality and legitimacy of the arbitration procedure, various issues must be resolved.

Arbitration is governed by the Act on Arbitration and the Polish Code of Civil Procedure. With a robust legal system and skilled practitioners, the nation has a well-developed mechanism for arbitrating conflicts.

Commercial conflicts, construction disputes, and intellectual property disputes are among the disputes that are settled by arbitration. Poland has laws governing both domestic and foreign arbitration.

In Poland, an arbitration request must be made in writing and must contain certain essential information, such as the names and addresses of the parties and a description of the dispute. The parties may then decide to choose a single arbitrator or a panel of arbitrators or they may seek the assistance of an arbitration organization.

Poland has a number of arbitral bodies. These organizations support arbitration processes administratively and might also have their own set of guidelines.

The arbitrator or panel of arbitrators will hear testimony and arguments from each party during the arbitration process before rendering a binding decision to settle the dispute. Under Polish law, the judgment is enforceable as an award.

Generally, arbitration is a well-liked and successful technique for settling disputes in Poland, supported by a solid legal system and knowledgeable professionals.

Chapter 47. Arbitration in Belgium.

The Belgian Judiciary Code, which has special requirements for both local and foreign arbitration, governs arbitration in Belgium. The Law of 4 July 1972 on Private International Law is the primary piece of legislation governing arbitration in Belgium. This statute incorporates the well-known and most frequently applied UNCITRAL Model Law on International Commercial Arbitration.

Commercial conflicts are frequently arbitrated. The premier institution for commercial arbitration in Belgium is the Belgian Centre for Arbitration and Mediation (CEPANI), however parties may also select other institutions or ad hoc arbitration.

One benefit of arbitration in Belgium is that parties can select their arbitrators, who are frequently authorities in the relevant field of law or business. In Belgium, arbitration proceedings are often private, and the decisions reached during them are equally enforceable as court orders.

Parties may agree on the arbitration procedure in Belgium as long as certain legislative prerequisites are met. The arbitrator's jurisdictional authority must be agreed upon by the parties, and the arbitration agreement must be in writing.

An arbitral award may be enforced in Belgium if a party fails to follow it. Yet, there are very few situations in which a court can overturn an arbitral ruling, such as when it goes against public policy.

Overall, arbitration in Belgium is a recognized and well-established process for settling business disputes, and parties can profit from its adaptability, discretion, and experience.

Chapter 48. Arbitration in the Netherlands.

Arbitration is a well-liked alternative to litigation in the Netherlands. The following are significant components of Dutch arbitration.

The Dutch Arbitration Act lays the legal groundwork for arbitration in that country (DAA). The UNCITRAL Model Law on International Business Arbitration serves as the foundation for the DAA, which is applicable to both domestic and international arbitrations.

Establishments for arbitration. The International Chamber of Commerce (ICC) Netherlands, the Rotterdam Institute of Dispute Resolution (RIDR), and the Netherlands Arbitration Institute are among the arbitration institutions that have their headquarters in the Netherlands (NAI). These groups provide arbitrators' selections, administrative help, and arbitration rules.

Contract for Arbitration. All arbitration must have an arbitration agreement as its foundation. Under Dutch law, an arbitration agreement must be in writing and may be a separate agreement or a part of a contract. The arbitration agreement must include the subject matter, the number of arbitrators, and the location of the arbitration.

The parties may decide on the number of arbitrators by mutual agreement. If the parties are unable to come to an agreement, three arbitrators will be selected by Dutch law by default. Either the parties themselves or their representative(s) may submit a request to the arbitration institution for the appointment of an arbitrator. The arbitrator ought to be impartial and independent.

Guidelines for Arbitration. The procedures for the arbitration shall be governed by the arbitration agreement and the arbitration rules of the Institution. The arbitrators are free to conduct the proceedings as they see fit, subject to the standards of fairness and equal treatment of the parties.

Award. The arbitrator's ruling will be binding and enforceable against the parties. The award must be explained in writing and contain supporting documentation. The parties may ask the Dutch courts to have the award revoked if there are sufficient grounds.

A Dutch arbitration award may be recognized and enforced in other countries in accordance with the New York Convention (headquartered in New York) on the Recognition and Enforcement of International Arbitral Awards. Netherlands is one of the parties to the Convention.

In the Netherlands, arbitration is a well-liked and effective method of resolving disputes, and many companies choose it to do so.

Chapter 49. Arbitration in Switzerland.

Switzerland's friendly business and legal environment contribute to its reputation as a top arbitration jurisdiction. The nation's arbitration statutes are current and functional, and Swiss arbitral institutions are considered as among the best in the world. Some key components of arbitration in Switzerland include the following.

Legal System. The legal framework for arbitration in Switzerland is established by the Swiss Code of Civil Procedure (CPC). The CPC offers thorough provisions on both domestic and international arbitration that are based on the UNCITRAL Model Law.

The Swiss Rules of International Arbitration are the arbitration rules that are most usually applied in Switzerland. These rules are administered by the Arbitration Institution of the Swiss Chambers in accordance with the UNCITRAL Arbitration Rules.

Arbitration hearing place. The legal jurisdiction that oversees the arbitration procedures is determined by the arbitration's seat. The most popular locations for arbitration in Switzerland are Zurich and Geneva, which can be chosen by the parties.

Institutes for Swiss Arbitration. The International Chamber of Commerce (ICC), the Geneva Chamber of Trade and Industry, and the Swiss Chambers' Arbitration Institute are Switzerland's three primary arbitration institutions.

Award enforcement. According to the New York Agreement on the Recognition and Enforcement of Foreign Arbitral Awards, judgments rendered by arbitral tribunals with jurisdictional jurisdiction in Switzerland are enforceable. The provisions of the Convention have been incorporated into Swiss law by Switzerland, a signatory to the Convention.

Confidentiality. Due to Swiss law's recognition of the confidentiality of arbitration proceedings, parties may choose to keep the specifics of the arbitration and the ruling a secret.

Neutrality. One of the key factors making Switzerland a popular choice for international arbitration is its well-deserved reputation for objectivity. The country has a long history of political stability and is renowned for its impartiality.

In Switzerland, arbitration is a well-known and effective method of resolving disputes. Due to its institutional structure, legal framework, and reputation for neutrality, it is a popular choice for both domestic and international arbitration.

Arbitration in Russia is governed by the Federal Law on Arbitration Courts, which became effective in 2002. The law describes the processes and guidelines for domestic and international arbitration in Russia.

The arbitration may be carried out in Russia by tribunals or permanent arbitral institutions. One of the respected arbitral institutions in Russia is the Arbitration Centre at the Institute of Modern Arbitration.

The International Commercial Arbitration Court oversees overseas disputes at the Russian Chamber of Commerce and Industry (ICAC). Problems involving shipping are supervised by the Maritime Arbitration Commission of the Russian Chamber of Commerce and Industry.

Arbitration has, however, come under scrutiny in Russia. Others assert that the Russian legal system and judiciary do not always promote arbitration and the implementation of arbitral decisions.

Chapter 51. Arbitration in China.

In China, arbitration, an alternative to the conventional court system, is used to resolve disputes between two parties. The arbitrator is an impartial third party. Arbitration in China is governed by the Chinese Arbitration Law, which was revised in 2017 to clarify and streamline the arbitration process.

The two types of arbitration used in China are domestic and international. When there is at least one foreign party involved, international arbitration is employed; when there are disputes between parties within China, domestic arbitration is used.

In China, there are numerous arbitral tribunals;

Beijing Arbitration Commission, a significant body.

The China International Economic and Trade Arbitration Commission handles both domestic and foreign disputes (SHIAC).

The Shanghai International Arbitration Center is an additional venue for international arbitration.

In China, the arbitrator's decision is final and irrevocable and can only be disputed on a select few grounds, such as fraud or improper procedural methods.

Arbitration is typically preferred by parties in China to the traditional judicial system for settling disputes due to its superior speed and flexibility.

Both Australia and New Zealand often employ arbitration to settle disputes, and both countries have established legal frameworks for how arbitration sessions should be conducted.

The International Arbitration Act of 1974 is the primary law in Australia controlling arbitration. This Act establishes a thorough framework for the conduct of international arbitration proceedings in Australia.

In addition to the International Arbitration Act, each Australian state and territory has its own legislation governing domestic arbitration. Domestic arbitration standards and practices can vary greatly between countries and regions and are frequently not especially formal.

The Australian Centre for International Commercial Arbitration provides administrative and support services for both domestic and international arbitration proceedings (ACICA).

The major piece of law in New Zealand that regulates arbitration is the Arbitration Act 1996, which is based on the UNCITRAL Model Law. This law provides a framework for how arbitration cases will be handled in New Zealand on a domestic and international level.

The Arbitrators' and Mediators' Institute of New Zealand (AMINZ), one of many arbitration associations in New Zealand, is in charge of enforcing the AMINZ Arbitration Rules and providing support and guidance to arbitrators and mediators.

Both Australia and New Zealand have well-established legislative frameworks for the conduct of arbitration proceedings, and both countries often use arbitration to settle disputes.

Chapter 53. Arbitration in Canada.

Arbitration is governed by both federal and provincial laws in Canada, a country with a long history of using it to settle disputes.

The Commercial Arbitration Act (CAA), which applies to international commercial arbitration proceedings, is Canada's primary federal statute governing arbitration. The CAA establishes a comprehensive framework for international arbitration proceedings in Canada.

Each Canadian province has its own domestic arbitration legislation. These statutes, which are frequently based on the UNCITRAL Model Law, establish a framework for the conduct of arbitration proceedings within each province.

Well-known institutions for arbitration in Canada;

The ADR Institute (as it is usually referred to) of Canada (ADRIC),

The Canadian Arbitration (sometimes just referred to as the CA) Association (CAA),

The International Centre (ICDRC) for Dispute Resolution Canada.

These organizations provide support and arbitration services to parties seeking to arbitrate their disputes.

Arbitration has traditionally been supported by Canadian courts as a method of dispute resolution, as well as the legality and enforcement of arbitral rulings. Nonetheless, courts have the authority to overturn arbitral decisions if there is a violation of procedural or natural justice.

Arbitration is a well-respected and frequently used alternative dispute resolution method in Canada. Arbitration is usually chosen by parties because of its quick pace and adaptability.

Chapter 54. Arbitration in the Arab world.

Arbitration is a well-liked form of alternative dispute resolution in the Arab world. A single arbitrator or a panel of arbitrators may be appointed by the parties to a dispute to arbitrate it in a private, amicable manner.

Arbitration has become more well-liked across the Arab world as a result of its effectiveness, efficiency, and confidentiality. It is widely used in business litigation involving joint ventures, building contracts, and international trade agreements. By adopting arbitration, parties can avoid the potentially time-consuming and expensive judicial processes that could occur in traditional litigation.

Some Arab countries have enacted their own arbitration laws and norms to promote the use of arbitration as a valuable tool for resolving disputes. For instance, all arbitration procedures in the UAE are governed by the UAE Arbitration Law, which was adopted by the government of the nation. Both the Kuwait Arbitration Law and the arbitration law adopted by Saudi Arabia in 2012 can be compared.

Many Arab countries have also constructed arbitration centers to promote the use of arbitration and to provide administrative and logistical assistance for arbitration hearings.

BCDR, the Bahrain Chamber for Dispute Resolution.

The regional arbitration center for international trade in Cairo. as CRCICA as well.

International Arbitration Centre in Dubai.

Here are some illustrations of these facilities.

Arbitration is expected to grow in popularity as more parties become aware of its benefits as a form of alternative conflict resolution throughout the Arab world. The establishment of arbitration laws and centers in various Arab countries is a proof of the value and use of arbitration in the region.

Chapter 55. Arbitration in Africa and South Africa.

Arbitration is becoming more and more common in Africa and South Africa because it may resolve disputes swiftly and effectively.

Prominent organizations engaged in arbitration in Africa.

The International Chamber of Commerce, which has chapters in several African cities (ICC).

The UN Commission on International Trade Law is located at UN facilities in Africa (UNCITRAL).

the International Centre for Resolution of Investment Disputes, which has locations all throughout Africa.

Through the World Bank, state laws in Africa basically regulate the arbitration practices of all of these organizations (ICSID). The enforcement of arbitral awards and the conduct of arbitration proceedings are governed by these guidelines.

In South Africa, arbitration is governed by the Arbitration Act, No. 42 of 1965, which provides a detailed framework for the conduct of arbitration procedures. The law specifies the steps to be taken when choosing arbitrators, holding arbitration hearings, and enforcing arbitral decisions.

Particularly in the mining, engineering, and construction industries in South Africa, commercial disputes are regularly settled by arbitration. Conflict resolution services are offered to clients in a number of industries through the Johannesburg Arbitration Centre (JAC) and the Association of Arbitrators Southern Africa (AASA), two of the most well-known arbitration organizations in South Africa.

A few advantages of arbitration in Africa and South Africa are confidentiality, flexibility, and the ability to select an arbitrator who is knowledgeable about the topic of the dispute. In addition, arbitration is a popular choice for international disputes since, unlike court decisions, arbitration awards are often easier to enforce internationally.

Arbitration can be costly, and there is a chance that the parties won't always agree on the arbitrator to be selected, which would cause delays and increase costs. Notwithstanding these challenges, arbitration is a popular and effective method of dispute resolution in South Africa and throughout Africa.

Chapter 56. Arbitration is becoming more expensive.

Arbitration, which is an out-of-court conflict resolution process, can be a good substitute for litigation. It can, however, be a costly procedure. There are various causes for the potential rise in arbitration costs, including:

Rising need for arbitration services: As more businesses and people use arbitration to settle conflicts, there may be rising demand for arbitration services. As a result, arbitrators and arbitration institutes could impose larger costs.

Complexity of conflicts: Arbitrators may need extra time and resources as a result of the complexity of many issues that are currently being brought before them for arbitration. As a result, arbitrators and arbitration institutes could impose larger costs.

More emphasis on qualifications and experience: There are higher standards for arbitrators. This may result in more expensive fees for more seasoned arbitrators as well as higher costs for locating and employing skilled arbitrators.

Legal representation: Participants to arbitration procedures frequently retain expensive legal counsel. The expense of legal counsel may play a sizable role in the arbitration process' ultimate cost.

Administrative expenses: To pay the costs of overseeing the arbitration process, arbitration organizations frequently levy administrative fees. These costs can pile quickly, especially in complicated cases.

In general, arbitration might still be a more affordable choice than going to court in some situations. However, before deciding on arbitration as their form of conflict settlement, parties should carefully weigh the possible costs and advantages of arbitration.

Chapter 57. Steps to be taken to reduce the cost of arbitration.

Depending on the intricacy of the case and the arbitrator's fees, arbitration may be a more affordable option than litigation. The following actions can assist in lowering arbitration costs:

Choose a reputable arbitration provider. The regulations and fees for each arbitration provider vary. It's crucial to pick a service provider who can handle the disagreement effectively and affordably.

Properly drafting the arbitration agreement will help to guarantee that the parties agree on the nature and extent of the dispute, the number of arbitrators, and the amount of the arbitrator's fee (s). Later conflicts can be avoided with clarity and detail.

Employ a lone arbitrator: Compared to a panel of arbitrators, a lone arbitrator may be less expensive. Nonetheless, a panel of arbitrators may be required if the case is complicated.

Establish a budget: To help keep costs under control, the parties may decide to establish a budget for the arbitration procedure. Estimated costs for the arbitrator's fees, legal fees, and other expenses should be included in the budget.

Reduce the scope of discovery: In arbitration, discovery can be expensive. The scope and depth of discovery might be limited by the parties themselves or by the arbitrator.

Before going to arbitration, the parties may wish to investigate other alternative conflict resolution procedures, which may be quicker and less expensive, such as mediation or negotiation.

Ask the arbitrator to take cost-saving measures: The parties may request the arbitrator to take cost-saving measures, such as holding the arbitration hearing remotely, putting a time restriction on it, or following a more straightforward process.

Cost monitoring: Throughout the arbitration process, the parties should keep an eye on expenses and take action to stop them from rising excessively.

The parties can lower the cost of arbitration and increase the effectiveness and efficiency of the procedure by adhering to these steps.

There are other options to litigation besides arbitration. Here are some other options to take into account:

A neutral third party assists the parties in reaching a solution during mediation. As opposed to an arbitrator or judge, the mediator assists the parties in coming to a resolution rather than rendering a judgement. Arbitration or litigation may be slower and more expensive than mediation.

Negotiation: During negotiation, the parties may attempt to settle their differences amicably. Either directly or with the aid of legal advice, this is possible. A less formal and expensive alternative to arbitration or lawsuit is negotiation.

Expert determination: In expert determination, a decision is made by a neutral third party who is knowledgeable about the issue at hand. For disagreements involving technical or scientific concerns, this procedure is frequently employed.

Early neutral evaluation: During early neutral evaluation, an unbiased third party offers insight into the advantages and disadvantages of each side's arguments. This may result in a settlement and aid the parties in understanding their differences.

Mini-trial: In a mini-trial, each side presents its case to a senior lawyer or high-level executive who acts as the neutral third party. The impartial outsider then expresses an opinion regarding how the disagreement ought to be settled. Complex commercial conflicts frequently involve the employment of this technique.

Online dispute resolution: The parties to an online disagreement employ technology to settle it. Online video conferencing, online bargaining, and online arbitration are examples of this.

The best course of action will depend on the specifics of the issue and the parties' views. Each of these options offers benefits and drawbacks. When selecting the best course of action, it is crucial to weigh all of your possibilities.

Conclusion

Arbitration is an alternative to traditional court systems that involves one or more arbitrators making a legally binding decision known as an "arbitration award" to resolve disputes. This process is commonly used for commercial disputes, particularly in international transactions, and may also be required for consumer and employment matters under contract terms. It's important to note the distinction between mandatory consumer and employment arbitration and consensual commercial arbitration. While arbitration awards are enforceable in court, there are limited options for reviewing or appealing them.

Arbitration as a means of resolving commercial and investment disputes between parties from various nations is supported and encouraged by many international agreements. These agreements lay forth procedures for accepting and upholding arbitral rulings and provide arbitration proceedings a structure. The UNCITRAL Model Law, which acts as a model for national arbitration laws, and the New York Convention, which offers a system for implementing foreign arbitral judgements in more than 160 countries, are two of the most significant agreements. The International Centre for Settlement of Investment Disputes (ICSID), which offers specialist arbitration services for investment and commercial disputes, and the International Chamber of Commerce (ICC), which is well-known and highly regarded, were both created by agreements.

It's critical to understand how arbitration differs from other dispute resolution processes. The best process must be chosen for the specific disagreement at hand because each has specific advantages and disadvantages. Although mediation, for instance, entails a neutral third-party supporting discussion between the parties in order to reach a mutually acceptable resolution, arbitration, on the other hand, comprises a binding judgment rendered by one or more arbitrators. Parties can choose the most effective and efficient strategy to resolve their conflicts by being aware of the variations between these different dispute resolution procedures.

www.ingramcontent.com/pod-product-compliance
Lightning Source LLC
Chambersburg PA
CBHW070608220526
45467CB00003B/1343